DETAILED CONTENTS

Part I Creating Success in College

Chapter 1 In the Beginning... 1
The Stress of a New Situation 1
Quick and Simple Stress-Management Techniques 2
Creating a Positive Attitude 3
Activities 3

Chapter 2 First-Week Survival 4
Getting Ready: Preparation for the First Day of Class 4
The First Day of Class: Tips for a Successful Day 5
The Second and Third Days of Class 5
Activities 6

Chapter 3 Ongoing Survival 7
Nonstop Practice 7
Remembering What You Already Know 7
Remembering What You Learn 8
Communicating with Your Instructors 8
Building Relationships with Your Instructors 9
Communicating in the Classroom 9
Bringing Up Your Grades 10
Getting Help: Finding Tutors 11
Using the Library and Internet 11
Using Computers 12
Activities 12

Chapter 4 Confidence Building and Goal Setting 13
Steps to Increased Self-Confidence 13
Positive Self-Affirmations: What to Say When You Talk to Yourself 14
Goal Setting: Another Part of Success 14
Short- and Long-Term Goals 15
Measuring Goals: Using Time Limits 16
Rewarding Yourself: Developing a System 16
Activities 16

Chapter 5 Minimizing and Managing Stress 17
Managing Stress: The Benefits of Exercise 18
Sleeping and Taking Naps 18
Tips for Worriers 19
Taking Time for You 19
Activities 19

Chapter 6 Multi-Sensory Learning 20
You're More Than Your I.Q. Scores 20
Learning Styles Inventory 20
Scoring Your Inventory 21
Characteristics of Visual, Auditory, and Kinesthetic Modes 22
Using Multi-Sensory Learning 22
Developing Your Style: Combining V, A, and K Modes 23
Activities 23

Part II The Skills 25

Chapter 7 Getting Control of Your Time and Life 25
Managing Your Time: Why It's Important 25
Making Your Time Count: Determining Your Needs 25
Setting Up a Schedule: How to Follow It 26
The Weekly Schedule and Daily List 27
Procrastination: Dealing with Deadlines 28
Prioritizing: The Balancing Act 28
Identifying Priorities Exercise 29
Activities 29

Chapter 8 Developing Concentration 30
Tips and Tricks for Developing Your Concentration 31
Eliminating Internal and External Distractions 31
Getting Assistance from the People in Your Life: Helping Others While You Help Yourself 33
Activities 34

Chapter 9 Memory: How It Works 34
Short- and Long-Term Memory 34
Tips and Tricks: Doing What the Experts Do 35
Using Your Whole Brain 36
Hierarchies, Mind Maps, and Creating Pictures 37
Developing Your Photographic Memory 43
Tricking the Subconscious Mind 44
Activities 44

Chapter 10 Active Listening and Notetaking 45
Active Listening: A Great Beginning! 45
Preparation for Excellent Notetaking 46
Taking Notes 47
Establishing Your Consistent System 48
Short Cuts for Stressful Times 49
The Cornell Notetaking System 49
The Leonard Notetaking System 51
Activities 52

Chapter 11 Textbooks: Reading, Highlighting, and Notetaking 53
Reading Textbooks 53
SQ3R 53
Highlighting and Marking Texbooks 54
Taking Notes from Textbooks 58
Activities 59

Chapter 12 Writing Effectively 63
Getting Started: Prewriting Techniques 63
Freewriting 63
Clustering or Mind Mapping 64
Combination Clustering/Freewriting 64
Elements of Effective Writing 64
Beginning/Introduction 65

i

Middle/Body   65
End/Conclusion   65
Writing Research Papers   65
Preparing and Presenting Oral Reports   67
Group Presentations   68
Activities   69

Chapter 13 Test Taking   70

Test Anxiety: How We Develop Feelings of Panic   70
Preparation for Test Taking   71
Putting Your Skills to Work: Succeeding on Exams   72
Subjective and Objective Exams   73
Answering True/False Questions   73
Answering Multiple-Choice Questions   74
Sentence Completion and Fill-in   75
Strategies for Essay Exams   76
Writing the Essay   77
Activities   77

Appendix Time Management Forms   79

Index Inside Back Cover

PART I Creating Success in College

CHAPTER 1
In the Beginning . . .

I am always doing that which I cannot do in order that I may learn how to do it.

—Pablo Picasso, artist

You are beginning a new chapter in your life: pursuing a college education. Whether you are attending college to prepare for a career or to gain knowledge for personal development, flexibility and perseverance are essential for success. As you think about what you'd like to accomplish during your time in college, consider what you need to do to realize your goals. The information in this guidebook provides skills for studying and learning effectively as well as ideas to help you create a positive and successful college experience. As you try out new skills and test out ideas, keep an open mind. You'll soon discover which techniques work for you. We are capable of much more than we know.

The prospect of learning new information and acquiring skills can be exciting, yet daunting. Did you know that excitement and fear feel the same way in your body? Being prepared for what's ahead can lessen the fear of a new situation and help ease your entry into college life.

Going to college is not unlike starting a new job. When you begin one, you have to learn how to do the job, and your employer tells you what is expected of you. You "learn the ropes" and begin to build confidence in your ability to perform. College presents the same challenges. Once you learn how to "do" the job of school, you're on your way to success. Because you are the creator of your personal success, it will be your job to eliminate self-defeating behaviors that sabotage you or get in the way of achieving your goals.

Self-defeating behaviors are ones that defeat you and make success more difficult. Often people aren't aware of these behaviors because they have become habits and are easy to do without thinking about them. An example of a self-defeating behavior would be stopping work on a project as it begins to get difficult or close to successful completion. Procrastinating is another good example of a self-defeating behavior; time just seems to slip away and you're forever wondering where it went. Constant worrying and negative thoughts can nag at you and make you wonder if you are deserving of success. A self-defeating behavior is something that you *do,* not something that you are. Because you have learned it, you can change it. The "good news" is that you have the ability to transform negative beliefs into positive ones and create an empowering and rewarding experience.

THE STRESS OF A NEW SITUATION

New situations and environments can produce stress. College is an exciting place to meet new people and have new experiences. It affords an opportunity for personal growth and self-discovery, and at the same time, it can feel overwhelming, especially in the first weeks. Take your time, do things at your own pace, and most importantly, try not to worry. Trust yourself and you *will* build confidence. Think back to a time when you began a new project or learned something for the first time. You might have had fear or anxiety, but those feelings disappeared when you became more comfortable and sure of yourself. Remember that preparation can minimize the fear of a new situation. Here are some additional ideas:

- Talk to people who have attended your college.
- Check out your college's website, catalogue, and schedule of classes for information.
- Familiarize yourself with the campus.
- Expect college to be different from high school.

QUICK AND SIMPLE STRESS-MANAGEMENT TECHNIQUES

Because stress is a part of everyone's life in the twenty-first century, learning techniques to help you manage it can be beneficial. Many students not only attend classes, but also take care of families and work part-time or full-time jobs. Here are some ideas and suggestions for reducing and minimizing stress. Once you discover a technique that works for you, practice it as often as possible. The more you use the techniques, the faster they'll work for you. You will notice that most of these exercises involve deep breathing; that's because when we become aware of our breathing, it focuses us inward and generally slows us down.

- **Deep breathing:** The great thing about this technique is that it's easy and can be done anywhere. Simply become aware of your breathing and slow it down. Close your eyes and take several deep breaths. As you breathe, tell yourself that you are relaxed, centered, and focused. Open your eyes and continue to take deep breaths for several minutes or until you feel relaxed.

- **Progressive muscle relaxation:** You can do this sitting in a chair or lying down. Once you become comfortable, close your eyes and take several deep breaths. Begin by relaxing the muscles in your feet and ankles; the trick is to send your breath to the area that you are focusing on. Next relax the muscles in your calves and thighs, abdomen and chest, back, arms, and hands. Breathe deeply as you do this. Focus on relaxing the muscles in your neck, throat, and around your jaw (many people hold stress in this area). Relax the facial muscles, including the small muscles of your brow. When you feel ready, open your eyes. You'll feel more refreshed and less stressed.

- **Grounding or tree exercise:** Here's another technique that you can do anywhere. This one is especially good if you feel that you are moving in too many directions at one time. Begin by taking a few deep breaths; as you do this, pretend that your body is a tree. Feel the roots growing down from the bottom of your spine, down into the ground. Use your imagination. Now imagine that the ends of the roots are opening and that energy is flowing up through one side of your body and down the other, and then back into the ground. Do this for a few minutes and you will feel calm, centered, and "grounded."

- **Counting down:** This is another stress-reducing exercise that you can do anywhere with your eyes opened or closed. Begin by taking several deep breaths. As you breathe, count down numbers from 20 to one. Tell yourself that you will be completely relaxed when you get to number one. This is an easy exercise, and it truly does work.

- **Visualizing your perfect place:** Find a place that is quiet and free of interruptions. Get comfortable, close your eyes, and take several deep breaths. As you feel your body relax, imagine that you are in a place of total peace and tranquility. It might be a place that you've been to before, or one that you just create in your imagination. What's important about this place is that it's totally safe, stress free, and peaceful. Use your senses to really be there. What do you see, hear, smell, and feel? Walk around your perfect place. What do you notice? Each time you visit this perfect place, it will take you less time to unwind.

- **Additional suggestions:** Find a quiet place on campus for practicing a stress-management technique or one in which to sit quietly. The trick is to always go to the *same* place. Your mind and body get the idea that it's time to relax. If you have breaks between classes, walk around the campus at a brisk pace. Exercise is great for reducing stress. If the weather doesn't cooperate, find a place indoors to run or walk in place. The idea is to get your body moving.

CREATING A POSITIVE ATTITUDE

Our attitude plays an important role in our life. It affects our mood, energy level, performance, and health. What kind of attitude do you have? Do you look on the bright side of things, or do you find fault with everything and everyone? Now, think about your friends and the people with whom you spend time. Are they generally positive and fun to be around, or are they negative and "down" all the time? If you had to choose, which group of people would you rather be around? We tend to gravitate towards people who have a positive outlook on life. They lift us up rather than drag us down. Having a positive attitude can get you through difficult times and help you stay focused on creating success.

Suggestions for Creating a Positive Attitude

- Choose friends who have a positive attitude. Be aware that you *are* making a choice when deciding who gets your energy and time.
- Catch yourself when you have negative thoughts and change them into positive ones. Thought is powerful. Don't let negativity overpower you.
- Appreciate what you already have—the people and things. When negativity sets in, make a list of what you are grateful for in your own life.
- Become aware of the consequences of your choices. Do what's right for you.
- *Remember* that these techniques really do work!

ACTIVITIES

Activity: Progressive Relaxation

Directions: Have a designated group leader or your instructor lead you in the Progressive Relaxation exercise.

Leader directions: In a calm, modulated voice, say to the class or group:

1. "Get into a comfortable position and begin to take a few deep relaxing breaths."
2. "Notice where there is tension in your body and send your breath to that spot." (wait 30 seconds)
3. "Now, feel the muscles in your feet and ankles go loose, and relax." (wait 30 seconds)
4. "Now, let the muscles in your calves and thighs go loose, and relax." (wait 30 seconds)
5. "Let the relaxing energy move up into your abdomen and chest and feel the muscles go loose, and relax." (30 seconds)
6. "As you breathe, relax the muscles in your neck and throat. Relax the muscles around your jaw." (30 seconds)
7. "Now, take a deep breath and relax all of the muscles in your face, even the small muscles of your brow. Relax the muscles in your scalp." (30 seconds)
8. "Take a few more deep breaths and let any remaining tension in your body go." (30 seconds)
9. "Now, open your eyes." Wait about 20 seconds and say to the group, "How do you feel? Do you feel different than when you began this exercise?"

Have the group share their experiences with the class or in small groups.

CHAPTER 2
First-Week Survival

Don't overlook the opportunity to achieve something, don't be nervous, don't hold back; give it all that you've got, because the moment may never come again.

—Serena Williams, athlete

GETTING READY: PREPARATION FOR THE FIRST DAY OF CLASS

Feeling successful and confident on your first day of class can set a positive tone for the entire term. Here are some things you can do before classes begin to ensure a no-hassle, great first day and eliminate any unpleasant surprises.

- **Buy your books early.** Not only will you avoid long lines in the bookstore, you'll have time to preview the material and get a head start on the subject matter.

- *Preview* your textbook by spending a few minutes familiarizing yourself with the material. Glance at the layout of the text; skim the table of contents and index. Are there summaries, graphics, or test questions at the beginning or end of each chapter? You wouldn't want to take a cross-country trip *without a map* to guide you, so think of the preview as your map. How will you know you've arrived at your destination if you don't know where you are going? Previewing only takes a few minutes and it helps organize the information for you while you begin to absorb it; you may not think the information is getting in your memory, but it is.

- **Don't forget** to keep any receipts for books and educational materials. Bookstores generally will not let you return things without them, and on occasion, an instructor will change the textbook requirement at the last minute. Also, sometimes students find that a used textbook for the course will work just as well as the new one they've just purchased. Having your receipt will make the switch easier.

- **Buy parking permits,** bus passes, and meal cards ahead of time, if possible. You will avoid long lines that seem to be everywhere on the first day of the term.

- **Pay your tuition on time.** A student who hasn't paid *all* the required fees can be blocked from registering for classes. Some colleges will let you pay your tuition in installments.

- **Get to class on time.** Your professor will expect it. If you are using public transportation, know the schedules for buses and subways and allow plenty of time to get to your first class.

- **Remember that first impressions DO count!**

- **Locate** the offices of your professors and visit them before classes start to get the class syllabus. Once you've been on campus for a term, you'll have a good idea where offices are located. Instructors are in their offices getting ready two weeks before class. Why would you want to make a special early visit? Instructors have many students each term and do not always have the time to get to know all of them. Meeting your instructor before the rest of the class gives you a head start on developing a personal relationship. This can be helpful at the end of the term. Instructors tend to give students "the benefit of the doubt" when they know them. Introduce yourself and ask for a copy of the syllabus for class. Having the syllabus will give you an opportunity to discover what will be expected of you and what the exam schedule will be, and you'll have a great idea of what lies ahead.

THE FIRST DAY OF CLASS

Tips for a successful day:

- **Get to class early on the first day.** You'll be able to find a good seat and have plenty of time to settle into the environment and have the materials you need at hand.
- **Take a few minutes** to make a detailed mental note of what you notice, such as the size, temperature, and layout of the room. This is a great way to focus your attention and get ready for your instructor's first lecture. The first day is usually fairly easy; the instructor goes over the syllabus or course outline, tells you what is expected of you, and answers questions. Some instructors do begin lecturing on the first day of class, so be prepared to take notes.
- **Sit as close to the instructor as you dare.** This helps you concentrate by minimizing distractions in the room. Make eye contact with the instructor.
- *Read your syllabus carefully.* This is important! Your syllabus is similar to a legal document in that you are held accountable for all of the information in it. Your instructor has taken the time to write his policy for grading, absences, and assignments. Know it.
- **Check your syllabus** for test dates and immediately mark them with a yellow highlighter or brightly colored pen.
- **Look for the official date** to drop, add, or make changes in classes. Highlight that date. Remember that if you stop attending a class and forget to drop it, your G.P.A. (grade point average) can be affected.

The first day is the one in which to have all of your questions answered. Students sometimes wait for others to do this. If you are uncomfortable asking your instructor a question in class, use her office hours to make a personal visit. Having all of the information you need is the best way to begin the term.

- If you are unable to attend class on the first day, call the instructor ahead of time and let him know your circumstances. Some colleges allow instructors to drop students if they don't attend the first day of class. This makes the class available for students who are waiting to get in.
- If you are trying to get into a class that is full, talk with the instructor and let her know that you want to be in it. Make arrangements to get on a waiting list and to sit in even if you are not officially registered. Students often drop classes by the end of the first week. Don't give up! Persistence and motivation count.
- During the class, take the best notes that you can. Don't worry if you don't get everything in the instructor's lecture. You *will* get better with practice. After you've attended your first day of classes, and before you go home, make copies of the assignment form located in the back of this book. This page is used to keep track of your assignments and the dates they are due. Make several copies for each class to use throughout the term. During a break between classes, read over any notes that you have written in class. Reading your notes every day helps you learn and improve your memory. The first day of class sets the tone for the term, so using it to organize your assignments, notebooks, and materials is essential.
- Begin reading your assignments and studying immediately.

THE SECOND AND THIRD DAYS OF CLASS

By the second and third days, you will be able to determine the pace of a class. This information can assist you in setting up daily study schedules. You'll also discover the lecturing style of your instructor, which will help you adjust your notetaking pace. You'll also learn more of what is expected of you. Although some instructors don't mind students conversing quietly about the material, others demand a quiet classroom. Some instructors will want you to raise your hand to be called on, whereas others will let people speak out when they have something to say. One instructor might take attendance and consider it important, whereas another does not. Again, it's up to you to simply pay attention as the rules are revealed.

- During the first week, it's important to attend every class and to get organized. Keep a separate notebook for each class, with study and assignment sheets readily available, because you'll be checking off assignments as you complete them.
- Keep your assignment sheet as the first page in your notebook. Make an extra copy to post on your home bulletin board or for your special study area.
- Use your computer to help organize your assignments. Use spread sheets, calendars, and e-mail alerts. Knowing when an assignment is due gives you a time reference.

Life doesn't always go as smoothly as we like, and when unexpected things happen during the first week of classes, problem-solving techniques can bring positive solutions to dilemmas. What would you do if:

1. You have a family emergency and you have to miss a class the first week?
2. You discover that you have not received your student loan money in time to pay your tuition?
3. You lose your books and notebooks?
4. After being in class, you feel that you won't be able to do the required work?

The answer is *don't panic!* Learning to solve problems in a calm manner can go a long way towards achieving your desired results.

ACTIVITIES

Activity 1: Problem Solving the Unexpected

Directions: Take each of the situations listed above and write your own solutions below.

1. _____
   _____
2. _____
   _____
3. _____
   _____
4. _____
   _____

I'm sure that you came up with great answers. The important thing to remember is that there is always someone at your college who can assist you when you need help. It could be (1) an instructor, (2) a financial-aid counselor, (3) the person who works in the "Lost and Found," or (4) a tutor or school counselor. The people working at your school are being paid to help you.

Activity 2: Checklist: End of the First Week

Directions: Check all of the boxes that apply.

❏ 1. I've read and thoroughly understand the class syllabus.
❏ 2. I know the names of my instructors and their phone numbers and e-mail addresses.
❏ 3. I know the office hours for each of my instructors.
❏ 4. I attended every class of the first week.
❏ 5. I've purchased books for all of my classes.
❏ 6. I've charted the due dates for all of my assignments.
❏ 7. I've previewed the texts and materials for all of my classes.

- 8. I have a three-ring binder (notebook) for each class I am taking.
- 9. I have assignment sheets in the front of each notebook.
- 10. I have completed all of the assignments for the first week.

CHAPTER 3
Ongoing Survival

All serious daring starts from within.

—Eudora Welty, author

NONSTOP PRACTICE

Do you remember the first time you drove a car or learned to play a musical instrument? You might have felt awkward as you lifted one foot off the clutch while the other pressed down on the gas pedal. Think back to the way your fingers felt as you put them on the fret board of the guitar and formed a chord. Can you remember when you first learned to play a sport? If you wanted to excel at it, practicing was certainly required. Learning new information also requires ongoing practice. Studying every day helps you retain information and store it in your memory. When you are prepared, you feel more confident. Confidence creates success, which creates more confidence, which creates more success. You get the idea. (See Figure 3.1.)

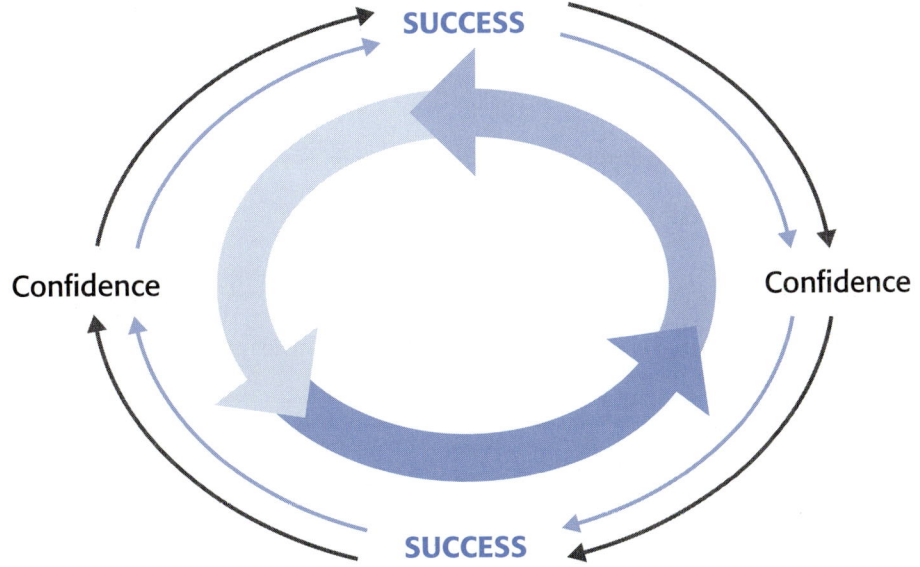

Figure 3.1

It's a positive cycle and you *can* create it! Ongoing practice helps you turn good study habits into lifelong learning. Because we humans are creatures of habit, the trick is to create good habits rather than self-defeating ones. We want to use our habitual nature to our advantage.

REMEMBERING WHAT YOU ALREADY KNOW

Your memory is like a bank. You deposit information into it and when you need to remember something, you make a withdrawal. The part of your memory that stores the information is called the long-term memory, and has the capacity to store infinite amounts of information. You already have knowledge stored; in fact, you know more than you think you do. All of your experiences in life have given you knowledge, and in college, this is a valuable resource.

REMEMBERING WHAT YOU LEARN

You can use what you already know as a basis for new knowledge. Think of a pyramid; the base needs to be strong to hold up the entire structure. Building a strong foundation of knowledge will serve you in the future. The Great Pyramid in Egypt took many years of painstaking labor to build, but the structure still stands today, thousands of years later.

When you learn new information, try to connect it to something you already know. This will help you remember it. Be an active learner. Get involved with the material. Remember that your memory "bank" is already rich. (See Figure 3.2.)

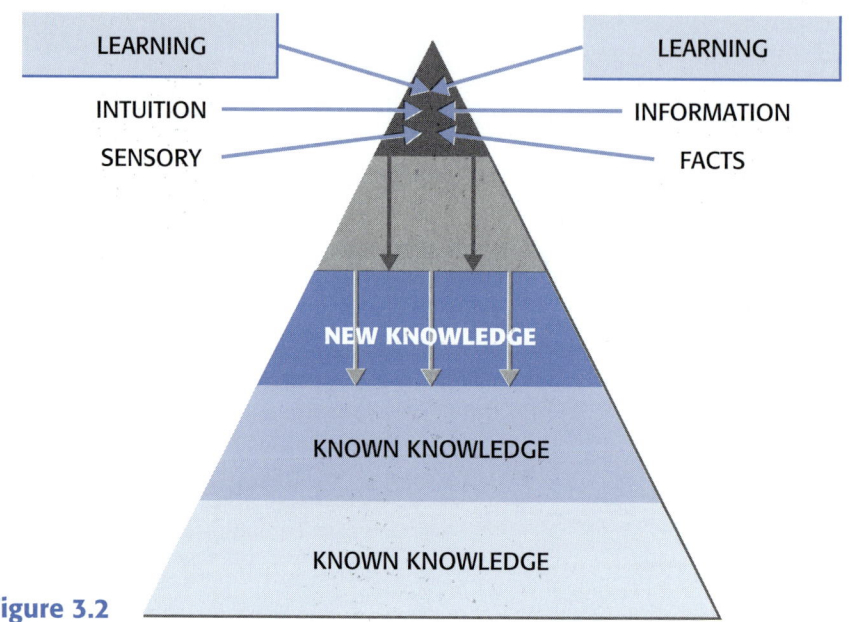

Figure 3.2

COMMUNICATING WITH YOUR INSTRUCTORS

In college, learning to communicate with an instructor is as important as attending class. It is the instructor who answers questions, clarifies information, and makes decisions that can benefit you. Good communication can reduce your stress and eliminate unnecessary fear and worry.

Tips for communicating with your instructors:

- **If you communicate by phone,** be sure to clearly state your name, phone number, the time and date you are calling, the best time you can be reached, and the purpose or your call. Playing phone tag with an instructor hurts you; you're the one needing the assignment.
- If you use e-mail and don't hear from your instructor within a day or two, **follow up with a phone call.** State that you previously sent him a message through e-mail. If you leave him a note, write legibly and leave your phone number and the best time you can be reached.
- **Develop positive interaction with your instructor.** An instructor who knows and likes a student tends to give him or her "the benefit of the doubt."
- **When asking a question during class,** be as specific as possible. If you still don't understand after your question was answered, make an appointment to talk with your instructor during office hours. A one-on-one session might be exactly what you need to fully understand the material.
- If you are not happy with a grade you received, do not bring up the issue while class is in session. Make an appointment to talk with your instructor during office hours. **Don't complain**

about your grade, but *do* ask what you can do to improve your score in the future. Don't be afraid to ask questions. Keep asking until you are satisfied with the answers. After all, it's your education. Most importantly, don't put off talking with your instructor; the longer you put it off, the harder it is to approach her.

BUILDING RELATIONSHIPS WITH YOUR INSTRUCTORS

Building positive relationships with your instructors enhances the teaching and learning process. Everyone wins.

- **Attend class regularly.** You benefit not only from the instructor but also from students who add comments and informative facts to the lecture. The instructor does know when you're absent. An "interested" learner attends class and participates enthusiastically. You can't get all of the information you need from a textbook.
- **Hand in homework on time.** This sends a message to your instructor that you are responsible and that you care about learning.
- **Come to class prepared.** You will get more out of a lecture if you have read the assigned material, taken notes on it, and are ready to participate in a class discussion.
- **Avoid excuses.** The truth is that instructors have heard them all! Honesty is the best policy.
- **Hand in neat papers.** A paper that has food or coffee stains on it does not send a good message. Be sure that your paper is easy to read. If it's not, it's probably not easy to grade.
- **Complain to the instructor,** not to other students. Meet with him after class or during his office hours. It's not appropriate to take up class time for complaining.
- **Always make an appointment** to meet with an instructor, unless she has designated "drop-in" hours. Meetings are usually conducted during office hours, but most instructors are flexible and will find a time to meet with you if you are unavailable during office hours.
- **Learn something about your instructor** and let him know something about you. This helps build a relationship. As previously stated, you are more likely to get "the benefit of the doubt" if the instructor knows who you are.
- **Don't take up class time** with a personal issue such as not being happy with a grade that you received. Make an appointment to talk with the instructor outside of class. Cancel an appointment if you know that you won't be able to keep it.
- **Use the instructor as a resource.** She may be able to guide you toward courses or give you the name of a tutor. Don't be afraid to ask questions. She has been at the college longer than you have, and can be a great source of practical information.

COMMUNICATING IN THE CLASSROOM

Getting involved in class discussions provides many benefits. It builds confidence that stays with you throughout your lifetime. It gives you the opportunity to become an active learner, which means that your understanding of the class material is deepened and reinforced. Participation keeps you motivated and interested in the material. When you get involved, you feel that you're a part of the class; when you contribute additional information, you help other students strengthen their understanding of the instructor's lecture. More importantly, instructors know who you are when you get involved. Whether or not participation is a grade requirement, the instructor will remember you at grading time.

Tips for participating in class discussions:

- Use **active listening** skills when another student is talking.
- Ask questions and listen to ones asked by other students.
- Don't interrupt, shout answers, or argue to gain attention.
- When it is your turn, briefly state your point. **Don't ramble.**

- **Keep your hand away from your mouth** when you are speaking so that others can understand what you are saying.
- **Stay on the subject;** don't tell personal stories that are not relevant.
- **Be prepared.** Read the material before you get to class and write questions ahead of time.
- **Clarify with a question,** and challenge in a respectful way. Use "I" messages instead of "you" messages. It's more productive to say, "I understand your point but I disagree with you because . . ." rather than say, "You've just made a ridiculous (stupid, dumb) point."
- **Make connections with other students.** Exchange phones numbers and e-mail addresses to keep you current in the class.
- If you don't like to speak up in class because you are shy, **talk to instructors when they have office hours.** Try to overcome your fear of speaking in class by practicing (role-play) with friends in a safe environment. When you feel brave, take a risk and speak up. Each time you do, it will be easier than the time before.

Do's and Don'ts for the Classroom

- **Show interest** in the subject matter. Be enthusiastic.
- **Ask questions.**
- **Give your attention** to the instructor and not to the clock on the wall.
- **Don't use inappropriate language in class.** What might be acceptable at home is not acceptable in the classroom. If you are not sure what is or isn't appropriate, ask the instructor.
- **Don't take up class time** with excessive talking about your own life and experiences. Keep your personal comments brief.
- **Don't sleep in class.** Some students work at night or have a special situation such as a new baby in the house. If you're having trouble staying awake, talk to the instructor.
- **Don't side talk.** Talk to your classmates when it's appropriate, such as in group assignments or class discussions, not when the instructor is giving a lecture.

BRINGING UP YOUR GRADES

During the term, you may discover that your grade in a class isn't what you thought it would be. Rather than spending time feeling disappointed, take action and try to change it before the end of the term.

- **Talk with your instructor** and find out if he accepts extra-credit work. Some instructors will allow it, but others frown upon it.
- **Add extra study hours** to your schedule. Cut out a social activity for a short while, until your grades improve. You don't have to cut out the activity forever.
- **Use more weekend time to study.** Set your alarm clock and get up an hour earlier than you normally do.
- **Talk to classmates** and form a study group, or join one that is already in progress.
- **Sign up to get a tutor.** Most colleges offer free tutoring services to students. Check with your specific department, or locate a tutoring center on campus through the college directory or website.
- **Find out** which students in your class got A's on the last test and ask them if they would be willing to study with you. This suggestion might require some bravery on your part.
- **Don't wait until the end of the term to get help.** Secure help as soon as you feel you are not understanding the class material or not getting the grades that you want. Things generally do not get better by themselves. Taking action at the beginning of the term can make the difference in your grade.
- If you are working at a job, try to cut a few hours on a short-term basis. Of course, this is not always possible. **Talk to your boss.** Perhaps you could trade hours with another employee as it gets close to exam time.

GETTING HELP: FINDING TUTORS

It's OK to ask for help. Don't wait until it's too late to benefit from tutoring. If you decide to utilize the services at your college, work with a person with whom you are comfortable.

- **Ask your instructor** to provide extra help. Most instructors are happy to give you time during office hours. Set up an appointment rather than just drop in.
- **Keep your tutoring appointments** and always arrive on time.
- **Take responsibility** for getting the help you need. Don't depend on your instructor or parent to set up the first meeting.
- **Hire a tutor.** College students offer tutoring services for minimal fees. Check school bulletin boards and ask department representatives if they can give you names of people who can help you.
- If free tutoring services are not available and you cannot afford to hire someone, **try offering a work exchange.** What skills do you have? Can you do carpentry, cook, or baby-sit? The barter system is beneficial for you and the tutor.
- **Parents, relatives, friends, and neighbors** can be a resource for you. Use these personal resources to create success.

USING THE LIBRARY AND THE INTERNET

The campus library is a valuable resource for finding information that you will need for research. Campus libraries provide a varied source of materials including books, periodicals, current newspapers, magazines, journals, and computers for Internet access. Additional library resources include a media section containing audio and videotapes, records, laser discs, and CD-ROM databases such as ERIC, EBSCO, SIRS, and MEDLINE.

The library also offers indexes to well-known papers such as the *New York Times* and the *Washington Post*, local newspapers, telephone directories, magazine indexes such as *The Reader's Guide to Periodical Literature*, and specialized journals and abstracts.

Reference materials include encyclopedias, dictionaries, thesauruses, government documents, and atlases. Check out www.Refdesk.com and www.ipl.org (Internet public library).

Using the library has several advantages. Besides being the best place to research material, it's a great quiet place to study or to relax with a newspaper or magazine. Familiarize yourself with the library and all it has to offer—it can be a great "friend" to you.

Tips for using information resources:

- **Take a library tour early in your college career.** Most campuses offer tours or classes for freshman groups; some have orientation classes that include a library visit. If your college doesn't offer a class, and you tour solo, be sure to ask for informational handouts that you can keep in your notebook for reference.
- **Don't be afraid to ask a librarian for help.** Remember that they have degrees in library science, and it's their job to know how to help you. You're not expected to know where everything is located.
- **Use the library for studying.** Because it's a quiet environment, you can concentrate with minimal distractions while respecting the right of others to study quietly, too.
- **Libraries have different classification systems.** Find out which one is used by your college. An online catalogue will let you search for books by entering the title of the book, the author's name, the subject of interest, or key words.
- Most colleges now offer Internet accounts for students. Open an account early in the term. Search engines will help you locate information. **Google, Alta Vista, Dogpile, Ask Jeeves, Excite, HotBot, Lycos, AllTheWeb,** and **Profusion** are current popular sites.

USING COMPUTERS

Colleges now have computers for student use; however, there may be a fee involved, which can be hourly, monthly, or by the term. Often, fees are collected as part of tuition. Check the policy at your campus.

- When using computers, keep the disks you use with you. *Always* back up everything you write. When you print a completed assignment, make an extra copy and keep it in your notebook. Instructors do misplace papers, and if there is a discrepancy about your grade, you will have the copy to turn in, showing that the work was done. Keep all of your papers until you have your final grade.

- Don't depend on using a friend's computer unless he or she is reliable; it may not be available when you need to use it. Working around someone else's schedule can be stressful.

- If you decide to buy a computer, check the college bookstore for student specials and discounts. People are continually upgrading their computers and printers as technology changes, so there is a market for used equipment. College and local newspapers are good sources to check, as well as the Internet. Ask your friends and instructors if they know of anyone selling a computer. Word of mouth is a great way to find out what's available.

- The public libraries in your area should have computers available for use, although the hours may be more limited than the ones on campus.

ACTIVITIES

Activity 1: Learning to Research

Directions: Choose a topic of your choice or one that your instructor assigns. Find three different sources of information related to your topic from:

1. A current magazine (periodical) or newspaper,
2. An Internet source from your college's database, and
3. A book from the library.

Write a short description of the information that you found from each source.

Activity 2: Using the Internet

Directions: Use the Internet to locate:

1. The movie schedule at a local theatre,
2. An urban legend,
3. A current local news story,
4. The names of the governor, senator, and representatives of your state, and
5. Information about your favorite musical group.

Activity 3: Finding the Tutoring Center

Directions: Locate the tutoring or learning center on your campus. Use the telephone or the college's website to gather information. What are the center's hours? How often are tutors available to help you? How much time can each one spend with you? How do you sign up for a tutor?

Write the information in your notebook for future use.

CHAPTER 4
Confidence Building and Goal Setting

You have to believe in yourself in spite of what other people believe.

—Whoopi Goldberg

STEPS TO INCREASED SELF-CONFIDENCE

Self-esteem can be defined as how you feel about yourself. It is your self-image. If you have high self-esteem, you have a positive self-image and feel that you are a worthwhile and deserving person. You have faith in your abilities and trust that you make the right decisions for yourself. If you have low self-esteem, you have a low opinion of yourself and a negative self-image. You tend to trust and have faith in other people more than you do yourself. How can you build self-esteem and change a negative image into a positive one? One way is to develop confidence in your own abilities. This may seem like an insurmountable task if you already feel bad about yourself, but the "good news" is that you can change an old pattern of negative beliefs and build confidence to achieve success in school and in life.

Where do the ideas we have about ourselves come from? We begin to develop our self-image in childhood, depending upon the messages we receive from our parents and people around us. As children, we believe what people tell us about ourselves. Depending upon the message, the effects are positive or negative. If we hear that we are lazy and that we can't do anything right, or that we'll never amount to anything, we feel bad inside and can carry these feelings into adulthood. The task then is to change the message to one that is positive and self-empowering.

When you feel successful, you feel more confident, which opens the way to more success. It's a positive, self-affirming cycle. Here are some tips to follow and ideas to consider. Some of the suggested tips may be difficult to follow at first, but with practice, positive, successful changes will occur. Remember that you can take action immediately.

- Don't let others define you. Well-intentioned friends and family may have preconceived ideas about you. For various reasons, they think they know what you can, can't, and should do. **The *only* person who can define you is you.** You are your best resource.
- **Avoid negative people.** Some people always see the negative side of a situation. They will not help you increase your self-confidence; in fact, they can undermine it. Their behavior can alter your mood and affect you emotionally. You end up feeling worn down. Positive people, on the other hand, are easy to be around and will be encouraging and uplifting. They want to see you confident and successful.
- **Accept the small successes.** Although we are often successful in our daily lives, we often ignore or minimize "little successes." Here's an example: A student participates in a class discussion and earns a compliment from the instructor; he pretends that it doesn't mean anything. Another student is tired and doesn't feel like attending class, but he pushes himself to get there and takes good notes for the day. Don't gloss over the "little successes," because they help you build your confidence. They do add up to bigger successes.
- **Write a short daily list** of several things that you can do each day to build your self-esteem. Keep the list with you and look at it to remind you of what is important in building your confidence.

- **Follow through on tasks.** Accomplishing what you've set out to do is a great success builder. Do what is designated on your time-management schedule. Staying on task to reach a goal gives you confidence to move to something more challenging.
- **Take care of yourself physically, mentally, and emotionally.** This book has many suggestions for creating your well-being.

POSITIVE SELF-AFFIRMATIONS: WHAT TO SAY WHEN YOU TALK TO YOURSELF

Affirmations are statements using positive language. If you have heard someone answer a question with "Affirmative!" instead of a simple "yes," you know the power of that word. It seems charged with energy. There isn't any doubt in that response. *Self-affirmations* are positive statements that you say to yourself. Most people don't think that they talk to themselves, but we do it all the time. Stop yourself during the course of your day and pay attention to what's going on in your mind. What do you say to yourself? Is it, "I'll never have enough time to complete this assignment," or "This is so hard," or "I'm going to be late for class—I'm always late." When we talk to ourselves (mind chatter), we give messages to a deep part of our mind, the subconscious. We are not aware of this part of the mind, yet it accepts what we say and believes our statements to be true. The subconscious mind is discussed in more detail in Chapter 9 on memory, but for now, think of it as a receptacle. What do you want to put in it? Positive thoughts or negative ones? It makes sense to think positively when we know that what we say to ourselves has an impact. It really does matter! How can we change the negative statements above to positive ones? "I'll never have enough time to complete this assignment" could be changed to, "I have enough time to complete this assignment." "This is so hard" could be changed to, "This is getting easier every day." Are you too familiar with negative mind chatter? Changing how you think might be a challenge, but it's one that will put you on a direct path to success. Practice putting your thoughts into positive language. Here are a few to practice on:

Negative Thought	Positive Affirmation
I never have enough money.	I always have enough money for what I need.
I can't concentrate on my work.	Every day my concentration is improving.
I'll never understand math.	_____
Life is really hard.	_____
I can't work and go to school.	_____
My kids are driving me crazy.	_____
I'm not smart enough.	_____

GOAL SETTING: ANOTHER PART OF SUCCESS

A goal represents something you wish to achieve in life. It is what you make happen. Remember that along with good time-management skills, "successful" people have goals. Success means different things to different people; whether it means having a 4.0 grade average, a dream job after college, a spouse and family, or traveling around the world, success and goals go hand in hand.

Why are goals important? If you answered that they help you reach your dreams, you are correct. The next question is, "How will you know you've arrived if you don't know where you're going?" or put another way, "How will you know if you're THERE if you don't know where THERE is?" Creating goals gives you the arrival destination and the plan of action that will get you there.

People tend to believe what they read more than what they hear. Reading what you have written is powerful; it makes sense to put your goals down on paper. It's easy to fantasize about all of the wonderful things that you want to have or be, but those thoughts will just linger as thoughts. Writing a goal down makes it more real and helps you focus on the daily and weekly tasks needed to make it a reality. It can help you stay focused when you feel overwhelmed.

When you have decided on a goal, the next step is having a plan for achieving it. This requires writing down each step that will put your plan in action. When you do this, you are on the way to achieving your personal success.

Tips for creating a goal:

- Write your goal in short sentences. Keep the language simple. An example would be, "I will complete my Writing 121 paper by Friday evening," or "I will complete my pre-nursing requirements by June 15 of next year." Put a specific date in your written statement.
- Write a goal that is both challenging and realistic. This takes a bit of practice, so don't worry if your goal doesn't come out exactly the way you thought it would on the first try at writing it down.
- Number each step in your plan of action. Write down the date that you will have the step completed. Target dates keep you motivated and focused.
- Use brightly colored pens to write your goals. If you like, use a different color for each goal.
- Keep your written goal in a highly visible place. Post it on your refrigerator, bulletin board, or bathroom mirror. Look at it every day as a reminder of what you need to do to get where you want to be.
- Break down your plan of action into manageable steps. A plan that is unrealistic can be a set up for failure, and that is the opposite of what you want to accomplish.
- Use positive language; your subconscious mind is taking in every word.
- Visualize yourself achieving your goal. Pretend that you have already accomplished it. This is an important step in realizing your goals. What do you see? How do you feel?

SHORT- AND LONG-TERM GOALS

There are two kinds of goals to consider, short term and long term. A short-term goal can be daily, weekly, or monthly. An example of a short-term goal would be to complete an assignment by a certain date or to receive a particular grade in a class. For example, if you want to get an "A" on a psychology exam, write your goal statement first: *I will receive an "A" on my psychology midterm exam.*

Next, write the steps in your plan for achieving the goal.

1. I will put in three hours of study each day.
2. I will make flash cards for each chapter.
3. I will unplug my telephone while I am studying.
4. I will ask Judy to study with me.
5. I will quiz myself every evening on the material I have been reviewing.

The process is the same for all of your goals.

If you tend towards procrastination, a daily list is helpful. If you need to, break down the goal into steps and check off each one as you reach it. Remember that "baby steps" usually work when nothing else will. As you spend more time in your classes, you will be able to gauge how much time you will need to complete an assignment. This information will help you write manageable goals.

Long-term goals are used for future planning. An example of a long-term goal might be to earn a college degree or to get accepted into a professional program. Your goal statement could be *I will be accepted into the nursing program by September of (date).*

The next step is to write the steps in your plan for achieving this goal.

1. I will take all of the prerequisite classes required for entrance into the nursing program by (date).
2. I will look into the availability of financial aid by (date).
3. I will apply to the nursing program by (date).
4. I will interview people who are in the nursing profession to get additional information by (date).

Because everyone has his or her own concept of time, a long-term goal is different for each person. For one student, a goal that takes three months to achieve may be short term while for another student, it fits the long-term category.

MEASURING GOALS: USING TIME LIMITS

Having a target date for achieving your goals is important. It lets you know if your time line is realistic, and whether you've given yourself enough time to complete the goal. It's like the "finish line" in a race; you want to reach it, but not at the expense of hurting yourself. When you achieve your target date, you feel successful and are motivated to accomplish new goals. If you don't reach your target date, don't panic. Adjust it to a more appropriate time.

REWARDING YOURSELF: DEVELOPING A SYSTEM

Rewarding yourself for reaching a goal is a positive behavior. Choose an activity that you enjoy doing, but don't always have time to do, such as seeing a film or reading your favorite magazine. If you're low on funds, check your college newspaper for free films shown on campus. Local theatres have inexpensive afternoon showings, or check out a free video at your public library. Your school library has magazines and newspapers to read, also free. Going out to lunch or dinner with friends is a great reward. Check the local listings for inexpensive restaurants and student discounts.

Even though you may feel great after accomplishing a goal, don't reward yourself with a big-ticket item like a vacation, compliments of your credit card. Getting into debt will create stress, and that is not relaxing. College students are always busy; taking the time for a relaxing walk or drive is a reward in itself. Often it is the small things in life that are the best rewards. Be creative. Catch up on e-mails and phone calls, or play your favorite sport. Only you know which is the best reward system for you.

ACTIVITIES

Activity 1: Writing Goals

Directions: Follow the instructions in this chapter for writing goals. Write one short-term and one long-term goal. List the steps that are necessary to achieve them. Remember to write a target date. Share what you've written with the class or in a small group.

Activity 2: Self-Discovery Letter

Directions: Pretend that one year's time has passed. Write a letter to your instructor, a friend, or a family member describing the wonderful, successful year that you've had achieving all your goals. Be specific and detailed. Date the letter one year from the day you write it.

Activity 3: Positive Affirmation Exercise

Directions: Follow the suggestions in this chapter for writing positive affirmations. Write three of them. Find a partner and read them aloud to each other. Have your partner acknowledge your statement by saying, "Yes, that's true" or a similar positive response. Take turns affirming your statements and acknowledging each other. This process is a powerful reinforcement of your success.

CHAPTER 5
Minimizing and Managing Stress

Adopting the right attitude can convert a negative stress into a positive one.

—Dr. Hans Selye, stress expert

Learning to manage stress can help meet the demands required of today's busy college student. Pressure can feel like it is coming from all aspects of your life. There are the deadlines for school assignments and the needs of your family, friends, and employer. Internal demands, the ones you create for yourself, can nag at you. One thing is certain; stress can affect your ability to perform well. It is difficult to study and concentrate when you feel anxious and stressed out; however, not all the stress we experience is negative. There is positive stress, too. Receiving a job promotion or getting married are positive experiences that can also be stressful. It feels great to get an "A" on a first exam; now think of the energy required to keep that "A" average throughout the term. Positive stress can be a great motivator. What are the positive and negative stressors in your life? Look at the example below and then create your own list.

Positive Stress
Learning a new skill
Keeping grades up
Planning a wedding
Buying a new car

Negative Stress
Assignment deadlines
Getting a "D" grade
Getting a divorce
Car repairs

Positive Stress
_____
_____
_____
_____

Negative Stress
_____
_____
_____
_____

Making a conscious decision about how you will handle your stress plays a role in minimizing it. When you take care of yourself first, you feel more in control of your life; it becomes easier to handle anxiety-producing situations. The trick is in learning to control your reactions to certain situations. Here's an example: Two students in the same class have studied hard for the midterm exam. They both want to get "A"s in the class. When the instructor hands back the exams, the students discover that they have received a C− grade. Student 1 is quite upset. He yells loudly, "Oh man! This can't be!" He is visibly angry and when the class is over, he sulks as he walks out of the room. Other students hear him blame the instructor, complaining that the test was too hard and that the questions on it were unfair. They hear him make derogatory comments about the instructor. Student 2 is disappointed by the C− grade. After class, he makes an appointment with the instructor to discuss his answers and to find out what he could have done differently. Student 2 decides to add another daily study hour for this specific class, and to look for other students with whom he can study. Although the same situation presented itself for both students, each had a different reaction. You can make a choice about how you will react to a situation, and that choice will affect your stress level. Although you may not have control over what happens to you, you *do* have control over your reaction. Watch your responses and try to become aware of the choice that you make in the moment. The awareness that you have will help you manage stress.

MANAGING STRESS: THE BENEFITS OF EXERCISE

Engaging in physical activity is an effective stress reliever. Often, students make a plan to exercise on a regular basis, but when they get busy and feel stressed out, it can be the first activity to get pushed aside. Instead, drinking coffee and eating sugary foods can become the "activity of choice."

Tips for incorporating exercise into your day:

- **Take a physical education class.** Most colleges offer a variety of physical education classes. If you enjoy athletics, take more than one class. If you don't particularly like to exercise, signing up for a credit class will motivate you, especially if the instructor takes attendance.
- **Check out the facilities** available on your campus. These usually have a minimal usage fee, or the fee may already be included in your tuition. Work out on your own time; the advantage is having flexibility.
- **Join a city sports team.** If you enjoy team sports, inquire into the city's offerings. Basketball and soccer are usually available. In the spring and summer, you can join a softball team. Local high schools and YMCAs are other places to check out.
- **Join a gym.** Private gyms have extended hours; some are open 24 hours a day. Would a late-night workout help relieve stress? If you are a "night person," you may prefer a 2:00 A.M. workout.
- **Exercise with friends.** They can help motivate you. If you are feeling tired and run down, call a friend; it's a great way to get yourself up and out of the house. Set a walking or running date.
- **Use a bicycle instead of a car.** If it's possible to bike to your campus, do it. Most city buses will have bike racks. Take your bike to school and ride around the campus.
- **Walk!** Walking is good exercise. The advantage is that it's free, and you can do it anywhere. Find a walking buddy. Discuss class material and quiz each other as you walk, or catch up on local news or gossip. Walk around the campus track.
- **Swim** at your campus, city pool, or YMCA. Schedule time for a swim between classes if it fits into your schedule.
- **When you are at home,** put on your favorite music and dance. Dancing is a form of aerobic exercise. Buy an inexpensive or "pre-owned" set of free weights. Use them to strengthen your body while you are watching TV or a movie.

SLEEPING AND TAKING NAPS

It's easier to handle stressful situations when you are rested. Getting an adequate amount of sleep is necessary in order to think clearly and to absorb information. Students often find themselves sleep deprived due to late-night study sessions. To stay healthy, you need to sleep enough hours. But how much is enough? It is important to determine how much sleep you actually need to function efficiently. Don't compare yourself to others. People have different sleep requirements. Even if you know how much you need, sleeping enough might be difficult. For some, falling asleep is a problem. If you suffer from insomnia, here are some tips:

- Get into bed one hour earlier than usual. Keep the room dark and do one of the breathing/relaxation techniques found in Chapter 3. Cover your eyes, if necessary. Eye patches used for air travel are sold in most stores. A soft cloth will work as well. Your mind and body will eventually get the idea that it's time to slow down, and a pattern will emerge.
- Turn off radios, TVs, stereos, and phones. Some students claim that listening to soft music helps them fall asleep. This will work as long as you are not distracted. If you find yourself singing along with your tape or CD, you probably won't be falling asleep easily.

- Count backward from 100. Take a breath between every number and tell yourself that you are getting sleepy. This is a good self-hypnosis technique.

Experts have varying opinions regarding the benefits of napping. Some say that taking a nap will interfere with your nightly sleep cycle and confuse your body, while others are in favor of taking naps. If you benefit by taking a nap, by all means, do so. The way a nap works best is to make it a fairly short one. If you wake up feeling rejuvenated and ready to go, your body is telling you that a short nap during the day is fine.

Some people seem to have been born with an ability to worry about everything. As hard as they try, they can't stop. If you are an excessive worrier, and want to change that behavior, here are some helpful tips:

Tips for worriers:
- Identify the importance of the topic about which you're worrying. Ask yourself if it is worth all the attention you are giving it. At that moment, choose to think about something positive in your life.
- Write down the problem or compulsive thoughts you have on a piece of paper, or type them on your computer and print a copy. Then write down the first feelings that you have. This doesn't have to take up much time. When you've completed this exercise, throw away the piece of paper. You are symbolically letting go of the problem.
- Talk to someone about your problems or concerns. Often, talking out difficulties with a friend or counselor can be needed short-term relief. You do, however, want to find someone who is a good listener.
- Do the five-minute worry exercise listed in Chapter 8 on concentration. This is a technique worth trying.

TAKING TIME FOR YOU

Taking time for yourself is essential to well being. Everyone needs downtime, whether it's ten minutes or ten hours. Taking time allows you to clear your head and gives you an energy boost. Determine how much time you can afford, and then do something that is just for you. When you take care of yourself first, it's easier to take care of others. Stress is cumulative, and sometimes we don't recognize its effects. Taking time is a way to reduce your daily stress level.

ACTIVITIES

Activity 1: Problem-Solving Stressful Situations
Directions: Write down three to four negative stressors in your life. Find a partner and share your list. One person will listen while the other person talks. With your partner, come up with solutions to help minimize the stress in your life.

Activity 2: Positive Stress Exercise
Directions: Choose a positive stressor from your list on the first page of this chapter. How will you use it to motivate you in the future? Answer by writing about it, drawing a picture or cartoon strip, or creating a collage from pictures. Share with the class or a small group.

Activity 3: Stress Busters
Directions: Choose one or two of the following "stress busters."

1. Exercise. If you already exercise regularly, try a different form.
2. Walk around the campus during any free time that you have. Breathe deeply as you walk.

3. Talk to a friend or professional about a problem.
4. Do something that you haven't done before.
5. When you feel stressed, say "STOP" to yourself and visualize a large red stop sign in front of your eyes.
6. Consciously change a negative response to a positive one.

How did the stress busters work for you? Write your response and share with the class or a small group.

CHAPTER 6
Multi-Sensory Learning

The best way to get a good idea is to get a lot of ideas.

—Linus Pauling, Nobel Prize–winning chemist

YOU'RE MORE THAN YOUR I.Q. SCORES

At one time, every student has taken an I.Q. (Intelligence Quotient) test. These tests did not always measure or recognize the full range of talents and abilities of an individual. Today's educators know that I.Q. reaches beyond test scores and that students have different ways of being "smart." Each student brings innate abilities, resources, experience, and potential to the classroom. One way in which you can reach your potential is to know your *preferred learning method* or "*style.*" This means knowing the way that you learn best. Learning involves accessing, processing, and retaining information.

The three main *learning styles* are *visual, auditory,* and *kinesthetic*. Although most learners use a combination of styles, one may emerge as dominant. Understanding the way in which you learn can make studying and remembering easier. The following inventory will help you identify your preferred style.

LEARNING STYLES INVENTORY

Answer the questions to the best of your ability. Mark a *yes* or *no* response.

	Yes	No
1. I prefer watching a video to reading.	___	___
2. When I sing along with my CDs or the radio, I know the words to the songs.	___	___
3. I have athletic ability.	___	___
4. I can picture the setting of a story I am reading.	___	___
5. I study better with music in the background.	___	___
6. I enjoy hands-on learning.	___	___
7. I'd rather play sports than watch someone play them.	___	___

Scoring Your Inventory   21

		Yes	No
8.	Reading aloud helps me remember.	___	___
9.	I prefer watching someone perform a skill or a task before I actually try it.	___	___
10.	I color-coordinate my clothes.	___	___
11.	I'm good at rhyming and rapping.	___	___
12.	I use phrases like: "I've got a handle on it," "I'm up against the wall," or "I have a feeling that . . ."	___	___
13.	I need to look at something several times before I understand it.	___	___
14.	I prefer having instructors give oral directions than written ones.	___	___
15.	I have difficulty being still for long periods of time.	___	___
16.	I use phrases like "I see what you're saying," "That looks good," or "That's clear to me."	___	___
17.	I'm good at figuring out how something works.	___	___
18.	I can understand a taped lecture.	___	___
19	It's easy for me to replay scenes from movies in my head.	___	___
20.	I enjoy studying foreign languages.	___	___
21.	I would rather conduct my own science experiment than watch someone else do it.	___	___
22.	I would rather paint a house than a picture.	___	___
23.	I enjoy studying in groups.	___	___
24.	I prefer to have written directions to someone's home.	___	___
25.	I can look at an object and remember it when I close my eyes.	___	___
26.	I have musical ability.	___	___
27.	When I study new vocabulary, writing the words several times helps me learn.	___	___
28.	I can imagine myself doing something before I actually do it.	___	___
29.	I use phrases like "That rings a bell," "I hear you," or "That sounds good."	___	___
30.	I enjoy building things and working with tools.	___	___

SCORING YOUR INVENTORY

Tally your responses by adding up only the YES answers. Put the number of the question in the appropriate box. For example, if you answered question number 9 with a yes, write 9 in the VISUAL box. If you answered number 11 with a yes, write number 11 in the AUDITORY box. If you answered number 7 with a yes, write 7 in the KINESTHETIC box. Add up the number of questions in each box and write a total for each one. This will determine your *preferred learning style*. Don't worry if a domi-

CHAPTER 6: MULTI-SENSORY LEARNING

nant mode doesn't emerge. You're a versatile learner! Use the knowledge you gain to create excellent study tools, the ones that are right for you. Chart your answers below.

Visual Style: Questions 1, 4, 9, 10, 13, 16, 19, 24, 25, 28
Auditory Style: Questions 2, 5, 8, 11, 14, 18, 20, 23, 26, 29
Kinesthetic Style: Questions 3, 6, 7, 12, 15, 17, 21, 22, 27, 30

Visual	Auditory	Kinesthetic
_____	_____	_____
_____	_____	_____
_____	_____	_____
_____	_____	_____
_____	_____	_____
Total:	Total:	Total:

The highest score indicates your *preferred learning style*. If you have a high score in more than one area, you're using additional modalities. Remember that there are no wrong answers to this inventory. Everyone is an individual and has her own style of learning.

CHARACTERISTICS OF VISUAL, AUDITORY, AND KINESTHETIC MODES

- **Visual learners need to *see* information.** If your preferred style is visual, you have strong visualization skills and can remember objects, shapes, and pictures. You learn by reading, and by watching films, videos, and demonstrations. You can see pictures in your mind.
- **Auditory learners need to *hear* information.** If your preferred style is auditory, you have a "good ear" and can hear differences in tones and rhythm. Reading out loud will be beneficial. You can remember what you hear in a lecture.
- **Kinesthetic learners need to be *physically active* and *doing things*.** If your preferred style is kinesthetic, you are a hands-on learner. You have good coordination and learn by doing. You generally have an active approach to learning.

USING MULTI-SENSORY LEARNING

Now that you know your learning style(s), you have an idea of the important role your senses play in the learning process. The best strategy is to combine modalities whenever possible. Incorporate visual, kinesthetic, and auditory learning into your study plan. Using combinations will strengthen your ability to retain information. Be creative. Add your own ideas. Here are some strategies:

Visual learners:

- Create mind maps, flow charts, and diagrams using bright colors. Put them where you can view them frequently.
- Practice building your visual memory. Refer to the exercises in Chapter 9 on memory.
- Rewrite your notes using different colors.

Auditory learners:

- After you read a page in your textbook, summarize the information out loud in your own words.

- Tape your instructor's lecture, and if you are a commuter, listen to the tape on the way home, either in your car, or on the bus or subway.
- Discuss the material that you have been learning with a friend or study group.

Kinesthetic learners:

- Use your hands. Cut up charts and diagrams. Create flash cards and move them around with large, sweeping movements.
- Walk and talk the information. Recite as you move.
- Type on a computer keyboard. You are using your muscle memory.

DEVELOPING YOUR STYLE: COMBINING V, A, AND K MODES

Additional ways you can use multi-sensory learning:

- Use background music (no lyrics to distract you) when you study. Choose a piece of music for a particular subject. Every time you study that subject, play the music. You are creating an association for your subconscious mind. You may be surprised to discover how much of the information you remember when you play the music by itself. You are combining V and A modes.
- Use rap or rhyme to memorize information. To add kinesthetic to this A mode, walk, dance, or clap when you sing.
- If you are athletically inclined, dribble a basketball while you recite information. You are combining A and K modes.
- Study with a partner or in a group. Discuss the information. Hold up flash cards, diagrams, hierarchies, and mind maps to test each other. This combines V and A modes.
- Put yourself in the picture. You can do this with a subject like history; participate in a battle or a significant meeting such as the signing of the Declaration of Independence. Ask yourself how you feel. This combines V and K modes.
- Make up your own strategies. Incorporate multi-sensory learning into your studies.

Additional strategies:

- If you are learning a new vocabulary word or math formula, write it in the air using large, sweeping movements. Close your eyes and see it in your mind's eye. Say the word out loud. You are combining V, A, and K modes.
- Use the sense of smell. One student created olfactory (smell) associations by using scented pencils for studying. He used a grape pencil for one subject and a chocolate one for another. When taking an exam, he used the appropriate pencil to help him recall information. He combined V and K and added an additional sensory mode.
- Use 5- by 7-inch flash cards to self-quiz. Use different and bright colors for each side. Lay them on a desk or table. Move them around and put them in different places as you study, or create a game with them. Place them into different categories in a hierarchical fashion such as "don't know," " review," and "need to study more."
- Create your own auditory notes using a tape recorder.

ACTIVITIES

Activity 1: Your Learning Style

Directions: Based on the learning styles inventory, do you agree or disagree with the results? Prove your position with examples of learning experiences from the past. Write your defense. Share it with the class or a small group.

Activity 2: Auditory Learning Exercise

Directions: From this or another textbook, select a significant section of information and create a rap or rhyme to communicate the meaning of the material. Perform it for the entire class, if you dare! This activity can be done individually or in collaboration with others.

Activity 3: Multi-sensory Lesson Plan

Directions: Select a favorite topic from your class and create a lesson plan for students using VAK techniques. Teach it to the class.

PART II The Skills

CHAPTER 7

Getting Control of Your Time and Life

Time is life.

—Alan Lakein, author

MANAGING YOUR TIME: WHY IT'S IMPORTANT

We never seem to have enough time. It's an elusive thing that slips from our grasp, causing us to ask the same question over and over again: "Where did the time go?" There are 168 hours in any week, no more, no less, yet we always crave more time, complaining that there aren't enough hours in the day to get everything done! Managing our time is important because it gives us authority over our lives and ourselves. We can't control time, but we can control ourselves by deciding what we do in those 168 hours every week.

In the many books written about success and how to achieve it, two main points emerge. Successful people manage their time well and set goals for themselves. (Refer to Chapter 4 on Goal Setting.) Successful students also manage their time well. They get good grades because they are prepared, know when assignments are due, know what is expected of them, and most importantly, know what they need to do to succeed.

MAKING YOUR TIME COUNT: DETERMINING YOUR NEEDS

The first step in acquiring good time management skills is to determine your needs. You find out what they are by taking an honest look at how you *actually* spend your time. Begin with the following exercise.

Step 1. Use one of the blank time schedule forms in the back of this book. For one week, keep track of everything you do with your time. Be honest with yourself. No one is judging you. The process is to assist you in creating a realistic picture of how you spend your time.

Step 2. When you have completed the form for one week, add up the hours and divide them into categories such as family, recreation, class hours, chores, commuting time, social activities, and work. Create categories that fit your lifestyle. Perhaps you have an ongoing weekly meeting, doctor's appointments, or a religious service that you regularly attend. You will want to include all of the activities on the form.

Step 3. Look carefully at your completed time sheet. What can you say about the way you spend your time? What decisions will you make based upon what you have written? After doing this exercise, some people make radical changes in the way they manage their time; others discover that they like things the way they are. Your determination is exactly that—yours! What works for you may not work for your friend. Don't compare your life to anyone else's; trust that you know what's best for you. You are now ready to take the next step for managing your time successfully—creating a time management schedule.

SETTING UP A SCHEDULE: HOW TO FOLLOW IT

Using your personal schedule is effective because it allows you to create a realistic approach to managing time and because it gives you flexibility, an important asset to have while going to college. When you have set aside time for a particular activity, you know what you need to accomplish in that time block. Because periods for recreation and socializing as well as study times are scheduled, you can focus your concentration on the activity at hand. It's a relatively guilt-free system. When you're spending time with your family, you don't feel guilty for not studying because you've set aside time for both important activities. Here are the guidelines for creating a workable time schedule:

Step 1. **Determine how many hours you will need to study for each class.** If you do not know how many hours you may need for each class, use the following rule: For each hour that you spend in class, set aside two for studying. In other words, if you have a class that meets three hours every week, create six hours for studying. You may discover that you don't need that many hours for one class, or you may need more. You can adjust your schedule as needed. This rule is simply a guideline.

Step 2. **On your schedule, write in the times of your classes and other activities that *will not change throughout the term*.** One example might be your work schedule or picking up the kids from day care. Now mark the times you will use for studying. Be specific. Write in "History 101" rather than "Study Hour."

Step 3. **Fill in the schedule** with meal and family time as well as time that you plan to socialize, exercise, or engage in any other activity. Check your category list.

Step 4. **Create flextime.** Flextime is a block of time that is open time in your schedule. You can block out one hour or an afternoon. You decide how much time you can afford and what you want to do in that time period. It could be used for studying, family time, or doing absolutely nothing! You can trade flextime as needed. Perhaps you have a midterm exam coming up; use your flextime for studying.

Additional tips for creating a time schedule:

1. Color-code your schedule: use bright colors—the brighter, the better. Choose a different color for each class and activity. Make copies of your schedule to keep in your notebook or day-planner. Put a copy on your refrigerator or bulletin board. This acts as a good visual reminder.
2. Create a schedule on your computer. This allows you to make changes when you need to, as well as print additional copies. A time-management schedule is not "written in stone." It may take some time to discover what works for you and what doesn't.
3. Trade time—don't lose it. Use your flextime or any free period to trade activities. The concept of "trading time" encourages a different way of thinking. Instead of feeling that time is lost, we gain it by trading one scheduled period for another. A regular Friday night out with friends might turn into a needed study evening as it gets close to exam time. As studying becomes the priority, students often give up TV time, computer games, or talking on the phone.
4. Schedule in weekend study hours. It's easy to forget about studying on the weekend, especially if you have been out of school for a while and have been working at a full-time job. Being a student doesn't end when classes are over; in fact, the work just begins. Another advantage to studying on the weekend is that it keeps information current. Repetition is needed to get information stored in your long-term memory.

Now that you've created your schedule, you will need to follow it for approximately three weeks. This will provide a test period to determine whether your time frames are workable and realistic. During the early weeks of the term, you're likely to have less homework. Remember to adjust your schedule as the term progresses because you'll be carrying a heavier assignment and study load. Following a schedule can be challenging, especially if you've never done it before; its function is to help you manage time well and to minimize stress, not create more of it. Be realistic and you *will* create good study habits.

THE WEEKLY SCHEDULE AND DAILY LIST

Use weekend time to create your schedule for the coming week. You might not have much of a change in your routine until you approach exam time. Since you already have scheduled times for studying, you can add additional hours. Getting up an hour earlier to study is a way to gain time. Write in the extra hour on your schedule, and don't forget to set your alarm. Be creative; move activities around when you have a busy or unusual week. *Always* add study time when you are preparing for an exam. Plan your week ahead of time.

A daily list helps you stay on track with tasks and goals. Make a list of what you would like to accomplish for the day. When you complete a task, check off the item. This is a great way to see what you've actually accomplished for the day. If you have difficulty in getting things done, a daily list is perfect for you. Use both daily and weekly schedules for effective time management.

Time tips:

- Ask yourself the question, **"What is the best use of my time right now?"** The answer may surprise you.
- **Use small blocks of time** that you might normally waste to review your class material. Do you spend 10 minutes waiting for your friend in the cafeteria? How about the 20-minute wait in the doctor's office or the 10-minute wait in the post office or bank? Three 10-minute periods equal a half-hour of study time. It's a good idea to always have study material with you. You never know when you may be able to take advantage of a small block of time.

Scheduling takes more time in the beginning, but the payoffs are great: good grades and accomplishing your goals. Figure 7.1 is an example of a weekly schedule.

Week of _____

Time	Monday	Tuesday	Wednesday	Thursday	Friday	Saturday	Sunday
6–7	Sleep →				→		
7–8	Breakfast & commute				→	Sleep	Sleep
8–9	History 101	Spanish 101	History 101	Spanish 101	History 101	Breakfast	
9–10	Psych 201	↓	Psych 201	↓	Psych 201	Part-time job	
10–11	Study Hist.	Study Spanish	Study Hist.	Study Spanish	Study Hist.		Breakfast
11–12	Volleyball	Swimming	Volleyball	Swimming	Volleyball		
12–1	Lunch				→	↓	↓
1–2	Study Psych.	Study Hist.		Part-time job	Study Spanish	Lunch	Flex
2–3	Writer's Club	↓	Writer's Club		Study Psych.	Laundry	
3–4	Flex Time	Flex time	Study Psych.		Read/Study English	Cleaning	Finish Eng. paper
4–5	↓	↓	Flex		Flex	Study Hist.	
5–6	Dinner				→	Study Psych.	Study Spanish
6–7	Review English	Write English	Work on	Study Psych.	Flex	Flex	Dinner
7–8	English 121	paper	English paper	Study Spanish	Socialize	Flex	Study Psych.
8–9		↓		or	with friends	Movie with Bill	Flex
9–10	↓	Flex	Review Spanish	Flex			
10–11	TV/Relax	Relax	↓				
11–12	Sleep	Sleep	Sleep				Sleep
12–1	↓			↓	↓	↓	

Figure 7.1 ■ Weekly schedule.

PROCRASTINATION: DEALING WITH DEADLINES

Procrastination is putting something off until a future time. Postponing tasks or assignments that need to be completed can create anxiety, especially when the task keeps getting delayed. If you are a procrastinator, consider yourself a creative person; after all, it does take some creativity to keep coming up with excuses. The trick is to take that creative energy and put it to work for you. People who procrastinate seem to like working under deadlines, which creates a kind of stress that would drive others mad. Whether you procrastinate regularly or on occasion, here are some helpful tips:

- *Stop thinking* about the assignment that you need to do and just begin to do it. For example, if you have a 30-page reading assignment and you find yourself sitting and staring at the textbook, *take action*. Open it up and start skimming. Turn the pages and let your eyes skim over the material. Now tell yourself that you will read five pages. After you have read five pages, tell yourself that you will read five more and then do it. The trick is to break down large tasks into manageable smaller ones. Imagine a large sandwich you're about to eat. You couldn't possibly put the whole thing in your mouth and consume it at one time; however, you can manage it by eating one bite at a time. An assignment that feels overwhelming can surely trigger procrastination. It *is* important to begin. Think of a popular shoe company's slogan and "Just do it!"
- **Set a realistic goal for yourself.** (See Chapter 4 on goal setting.) If you are tackling a difficult subject, allow extra time for the task.
- **Acknowledge** the work that you have accomplished. Don't "beat yourself up" for what you haven't done.
- **Work when you have the highest level of energy.** If you are most productive in the morning, tackle the most difficult subjects at that time. If you are a "night person" or you experience a "second wind," take advantage of the time to accomplish your work.
- **Try not to cram.** Cramming is an ineffective way to study and can inhibit storage of information into your long-term memory. Learning over a period of time using repetitive practice is a more efficient tool for retaining information.
- **Eliminate** external distractions. (See Chapter 8 on concentration.)
- **Change activities** if you are tired or if you begin to lose concentration. Instead of studying history for one hour followed by an hour of psychology, divide the time into half-hours. This will help keep you focused when studying becomes difficult. "Mixing it up" can be highly productive. Use a timer to keep you on track.

	Standard Schedule	"Mixing It Up" Schedule
1:00	STUDY HISTORY 101	Study History 101
1:30		Study Psychology 101
2:00	STUDY PSYCHOLOGY 101	Study History 101
2:30		Study Psychology 101
3:00		

PRIORITIZING: THE BALANCING ACT

Life for many students is a balancing act. Attending classes takes up only part of the day. Family obligations, work, friends, exercise sessions, recreation . . . the list goes on. It is clear that today's college students need to be good at "multi-tasking" and setting priorities. Priorities are defined as what is most important to you. Everyone's priorities are different. While family and church might be a priority for one person, sports and socializing might be a priority for another. Identifying your priorities will assist you in accomplishing your goals and in achieving success.

IDENTIFYING PRIORITIES EXERCISE

Write a list of everything that is important to you. Here is one student's list. When you've completed your list, look it over carefully and number each item in order of importance, with "1" as the most important.

Student Example 1	List your priorities
School (2)	_____
Family (1)	_____
Work (3)	_____
Friends (5)	_____
Exercise (6)	_____
Clubs (7)	_____
Worship (4)	_____

What did you discover about yourself? What is important to you? Prioritizing helps you put first things first. Knowing what your priorities are will be extremely helpful in this process. From now on, keep your priority list handy as a reminder of what is truly important to you.

Sometimes distractions get in the way of our goals. Here's an example: You are just about to study for an important exam when your friend calls to invite you to a party. She is insistent and encourages you to forget about studying. It's now up to you to make a decision based on your priorities. Do you want to go to a great party, or do you want to study for that "A"? Ask yourself what will get you closer to your goal. Remember your priorities when you are faced with tough choices. Think about why you wanted to be in college.

ACTIVITIES

Activity 1: Time-Management Schedule Checklist

Directions: Use the following checklist before you create your time management schedule.

_____   1. I have filled in the names of all of my classes.

_____   2. I have written in activities that will not change during the term.

_____   3. I have filled in meal times.

_____   4. I have filled in time I'll spend with family or friends.

_____   5. I have filled in time for recreation and/or exercise.

_____   6. I have determined how many study hours I will need.

_____   7. I have filled in specific study hours for each class.

_____   8. I have included weekend study hours on my schedule.

_____   9. I have distributed my study hours throughout the week.

_____   10. I have filled in flextime.

_____	11. I have color coded my time management schedule.
_____	12. I have a copy of my schedule in a visible place.
_____	13. I have made extra copies of my schedule.

Activity 2: Creating a Time-Management Schedule

Directions: Using the information from this chapter, create your first weekly time-management schedule. Follow it for one week. A blank form is provided in the back of the book. Review the example schedule in this chapter.

Activity 3: Journal Writing

Directions: Think of "time" as a precious commodity. Write about how you save it, how you spend it, and how you feel about it. Get into groups and share any discoveries that you made about your relationship with time.

CHAPTER 8

Developing Concentration

What we learn with pleasure, we never forget.

—Alfred Mercier, author

Concentration is the ability to focus without distraction. Have you ever noticed that you seem to have amazing powers of concentration when you're not trying to concentrate? Sometimes, the more you try, the harder it becomes. Think of a time when you were immersed in a favorite activity. The time seems to fly by; concentration is effortless. Unfortunately, this doesn't always happen when we are reading textbooks. Most students have had the experience of reading the same paragraph over and over again, wondering if any information is sinking in at all. Wouldn't it be great if we could transfer the focused concentration we have when we're doing something we love, to our textbook reading and studying? The key to accomplishing this feat is to *practice* the following concentration techniques. Create your plan and follow it.

- **Get into a routine;** this will help you concentrate. Study at the same time and place every day, if possible. Your time-management schedule is a good reminder.
- **Study when you are most alert.** Studies show that people are most alert one hour after waking up. If you're not rushing off to school or to a job, use that hour to study.
- **Create good study habits in the beginning of the term.** Remember that we are creatures of habit, and since it's easier to make a habit than break one, it's better to start out with positive behaviors.
- **Use affirmations.** Affirmations are positive self-statements. Every time you read or study, tell yourself, or affirm, that you have excellent concentration. Keep repeating this statement. Even if you don't believe it, your subconscious mind will! You are working with a powerful part of your mind.
- **Use the index-card technique.** Keep an index card next to your text or notebook. Every time that you begin to lose concentration, mark a check on the index card. By the end of the study

period, count up the number of checks. At the next study session, work at minimizing the number of checks you make.
- **Increase your attention span.** The trick is to PRETEND that the material you are studying is the most exciting and interesting you've ever read. If this sounds silly, remember that you are working not only with the conscious part of your mind, but with the subconscious part, which can be tricked into believing this is true.

Tips and tricks for developing your concentration:
- **Use relaxation techniques.** Practice the exercises in this book. When you are relaxed, your concentration is better. The *Deep Breathing* or *Tree Exercise* is an excellent one to do right before you begin your study session. Each time you do this, you will alert your subconscious mind that you are ready to concentrate.
- **Read with a pen in your hand** to help focus your concentration.
- **Listen to music.** Soft music without lyrics (words) can enhance learning. Certain classical pieces of music (such as Bach or Mozart) can actually change brain wave activity to help you learn better.
- **Create a study area and use it for studying *only*.** This is important because you are creating a positive habitual behavior. Every time you sit down to study, your mind knows that it's time to concentrate and learn. Your excellent concentration becomes automatic.
- **Have a desk in your study area** (no couches here). Students have come up with creative ideas for desks, including putting a door across two low file cabinets or sawhorses. Used desks can be found at second-hand furniture stores, garage sales, or through ads in the local papers.
- **Sit in a comfortable chair.** Put a pillow behind your lower back for support, if needed. Be sure to have all of your materials on your desk. This includes textbooks, yellow markers for underlining, notebooks, pens and pencils, calculators, and computers.
- **Be sure that there is adequate lighting in your study area.** You don't want to have shadows on your reading material.

The goal is to create an environment that is conducive to excellent concentration. Some students prefer to study in the school library for the sake of quiet and proximity to materials. If you live in a house that is filled with noise and distractions, consider using the library for your study area. If you do use the library, try and sit in the same place every time. When you are ready to study, whether at home or on campus, take a deep relaxing breath, tell yourself that you're going to have an excellent session, and sit down and begin. If, while studying, your mind begins to wander and you feel that you are losing concentration, *immediately* get up and do something else for a couple of minutes. Drink a glass of water or go outside for some fresh air. Go back to your desk and start the process over. Soon your mind and body will know that you are serious about concentration. Remember that these techniques require practice. Have patience, and don't give up.

Some Don'ts: Don't study in bed, where you sleep, or a table where you eat. Remember that you are creating a perfect study area, one in which the only thing you do is study.

ELIMINATING INTERNAL AND EXTERNAL DISTRACTIONS

There are two kinds of distractions—internal and external—that can affect concentration. The external ones are easier to eliminate. They happen in your environment or "outside of yourself." Outside influences can certainly detract from your ability to concentrate. What are the external distractions in your life? Examples are the telephone ringing constantly, loud music blaring through the neighbor's wall, dogs barking, horns honking, or roommates wanting to share their ongoing problems. What are the external distractions in your life? Here is one student's list of external distractions and her plan to eliminate them.

External Distraction	Plan to Change
1. Telephone ringing	1. Turn on answering machine, or turn off phone.
2. Family member always wanting to talk to me while I'm studying	2. Ask politely not to be disturbed, or go to the library to study.
3. Children wanting my attention	3. Keep children busy with creative project; or trade babysitting or child care with another student who has children; or spend an extra hour at school studying.
4. TV is too loud	4. Ask person watching TV to wear headphones or turn down the sound; or go to the library to study.

List your external distractions with a plan for change. *Hint*: Creativity plays a big part in doing this exercise. Use your imagination to come up with solutions.

External Distraction	Plan to Change
_____	_____
_____	_____
_____	_____
_____	_____

Internal distractions come from within. Examples are feeling tired from lack of sleep, experiencing hunger, illness, or constantly thinking about personal problems. Write your list of internal distractions with a plan for change.

Internal Distraction	Plan to Change
_____	_____
_____	_____
_____	_____
_____	_____
_____	_____

If you have a serious problem that is getting in the way of your ability to concentrate, make an appointment with a professional counselor. Your college may offer free counseling services. Check your local telephone directory or the Internet for names of local counselors who may offer a sliding-scale fee. There are many student service groups on campus, which can provide information. Talking with a counselor or teacher doesn't mean that there is anything wrong with you; it simply means that you

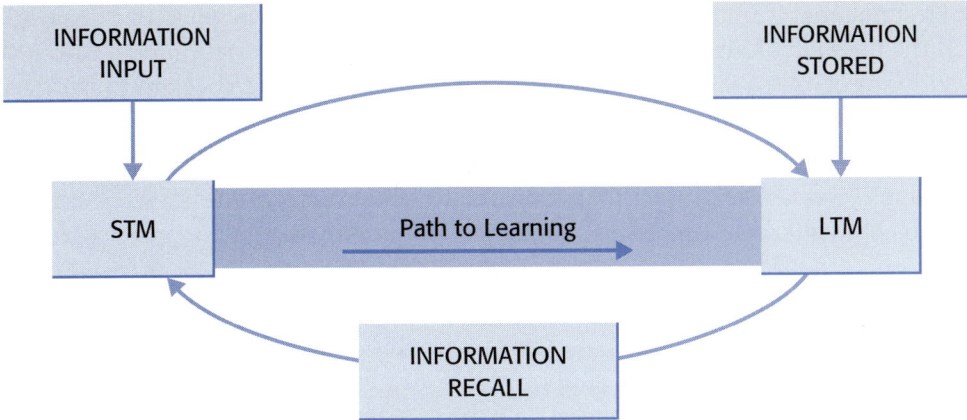

Figure 9.1 Short- and long-term memory.

chat briefly, but the following day when you run into her on campus, you have completely forgotten her name. You feel embarrassed. Blame it on the short-term memory. Here's another example. You are taking a telephone message. You have part of the phone number written down when your roommate walks in the door and starts talking to you. The number in your head completely disappears.

Memory is like a chain-link fence. Each link (thought) connects to another and creates a body of knowledge. This knowledge is stored in the *long-term memory* (LTM), which can hold infinite amounts of information. A student must store the material he is learning into the LTM in order to retain it and retrieve it on exam day. How is this formidable task accomplished? The answer is through *Recitation*. Reciting aloud is a powerful learning tool. When you recite the material in your own words, you are, like the actor, making it your own. In other words, you're not just memorizing the information, you understand it as well.

Additional tips:

- **Study in groups or with a study partner.** As you explain (recite) the material to each other, you begin to develop a deeper understanding of it. There might be gaps in your knowledge that can be filled in by your study partner or a member of the group, or you may be able to clarify the issue. Perhaps you discover that you need to review certain sections of your textbook. Each of you is processing the information through the filter of your own mind. Remember that *recitation* is important and helps you to truly know your subject.
- **Personalize the material.** This means putting your own personal stamp on information by effectively using study techniques that work for you. Because everyone processes information differently, a technique or skill that helps you may not be right for your study partner. Flash cards and mind maps might appeal to you, while outlines and copying class notes might appeal to your study partner.

Tips and tricks—doing what the experts do:

- **Use the principle of *Association*.** We remember things with which we have an association. A song from our past comes on the radio, and suddenly, we are singing along, remembering the words and experiencing memories. Emotions fill us and we're transported back in time. You will remember information if you create associations. Connect the new material with something that you already know. For example, if you have a geology class and you are studying rock formations, think back to the school field trip that gave you hands-on experience. What associations can you make? What do you remember? How did you feel when you were on that trip? ***Emotions and feelings are directly connected to memory.*** Use this knowledge to your best advantage. *Associations are memory links.* Connect the old knowledge to the new!
- **Use the principle of *Background Building*.** A subject that is familiar is easier to study than one that isn't. As a student, you will be introduced to many new and unfamiliar concepts. If

the subject material is unfamiliar to you, brush up on the basics. Begin with the glossary in the back of the book. Look up unfamiliar terms and write down their definitions. Check the Internet for basic facts related to the subject. Go to the library and check out materials that will help you get background information and build your knowledge base.

- **Use the principle of *Divided Practice*.** It is easier to learn and remember when your study time is divided into short blocks rather than long ones. Use the suggestions in the time-management chapter to help you create a schedule that divides your study time into appropriate periods.

- **Use the principle of *Selection*.** Making a good choice about what parts of your material to study is important. You can't possibly memorize every word that you read, nor do you want to. Begin by identifying the main ideas of each paragraph or section of the chapter. Think of a main idea as an umbrella. It covers supporting details, examples, opinions, and statistics, all of which expand the main idea. As you practice the principle of *selection*, you will be deciding which pieces of information need to be stored into your LTM.

- **Use the principle of *Visualization*.** When you use pictures and symbols to remember information, you are accessing the visual or spatial side of your brain. Visualization is one of the most powerful tools for memory. Learning visual techniques can improve your ability to remember, and the effects can be long lasting. Creativity plays an important part in visual learning; it can actually make memorizing fun.

An instructor shared the following true story with her students. The incident occurred during her high school drama class many years before. One day, a substitute teacher entered the room. Instead of taking attendance, as the regular teacher did, he asked each student to say his or her name aloud. This was a large class consisting of 35 students. When everyone had spoken his or her name, the room became uncomfortably quiet. The teacher then named each student, beginning with the first. The students were astounded by this feat of memory and wanted to know how he did it. The teacher then explained the memory trick. He used a visualization technique. As each student stated his or her name, the teacher created a ridiculous visual image and associated it with, or connected it to, the student. For example, if the student's name was Ben Waters, he might visualize "bending waters" and see a stream of water bending around the student. The water might be rainbow colors because color aids memory. The point is to create an image that is as silly or ridiculous as you can imagine. The more outrageous, the better! You are on your way to building visual memory. What images can you come up with for the name Carla Washington? How about *Carla* washing her car with a map of Washington state in her hand? Do you remember the famous picture of the first U.S. president, George Washington, with his wide-brimmed hat? Fill up the brim with funny-looking cars. You get the idea. Using creative and outrageous images will help you remember.

USING YOUR WHOLE BRAIN

Using your whole brain means utilizing both the right and left hemispheres of your brain. The two sides function differently, and learning how to incorporate both can create new options for understanding and for maximizing learning ability.

Left Side	Right Side
Logical	Intuitive
Linear	Nonlinear
Mathematical	Visual
Language	Spatial
Analytical	Creative
Reasoning	Subconscious mind
Conscious mind	

While we do use both sides of our brain to varying degrees, some people are more dominant in one hemisphere. Consider the artist who creates beautiful paintings, but can't balance a checkbook or keep track of his money. He sees the world in symbols and pictures and is highly intuitive about people. Would you say that he is left- or right-brain dominant? What about the accountant who is logical and rational and writes down every penny he spends? He won't make a decision without thoroughly researching a topic, and he would never make a decision based solely on his intuition. His home is organized, and he has a particular place for everything in it. Do you think he is right- or left-brain dominant? Of course, these examples are extreme, but they illustrate the differences in the way people think, and this has important implications for learning.

Traditionally, students have been taught using left-brain techniques. The teacher writes information on the board, the student copies it, and later, there is a test. Somewhere between copying the information from the board and taking the test, the information gets lost; it doesn't get stored into the LTM. This is a frustrating experience. By incorporating visual right-brain techniques, the problem can be minimized, perhaps even solved.

Making an emotional connection to information is a way to use the right side of the brain. We tend to remember experiences that involve our emotions. Everyone remembers where they were and what they were doing on September 11, 2001, the day of the terrorist attacks, but they would have to look at their calendars to tell you what they were doing on September 11 of the previous year.

When you are trying to learn new material, get excited about it, even if you have to pretend; remember that the subconscious mind doesn't know the difference and will believe it. Creating emotion and excitement is a way to remember and retain information.

HIERARCHIES, MIND MAPS, AND CREATING PICTURES

Hierarchies, visual memory aids, are also called Flow Charts and Tree Diagrams. The information you want to learn is categorized in a holistic way and is processed on the right side of the brain. You can make a hierarchy for a paragraph or a chapter in a textbook, or you can use it to brainstorm ideas. The beauty of a hierarchy is that there is no wrong way to make one. You are personalizing the information through your own processing system, your mind. Your hierarchy will look different than your friend's. Trust your instincts, and you will create a perfect one.

Because a hierarchy shows the relationships between main ideas and their supporting details, it is an excellent study tool. In a hierarchy, the most important ideas are written on the top levels (tree branches) while the supporting ideas get placed on the lower ones.

Begin your hierarchy for a textbook chapter by placing the main heading of your chapter on the top line. Use the next level for the subheadings. Under each subheading or branch, write information that supports the main idea. The trick is to be brief. Write key words and short phrases, which you will use to recall the material. Too much information will defeat the purpose of the hierarchy. As you recite the material, work from the top levels down. If you can't recite the information, go back to the text. Remember that *recitation* is the key to retention. You can create as many levels as you feel is necessary, but college exams usually do not ask test questions based on information lower than *five* levels down. When you study from a hierarchy, you get the big picture. All of the information is presented in one visual representation. Figure 9.2 is an example from a college psychology text reprinted in Figure 9.3.

Tips for creating hierarchies:

- **Use bright colors.** Choose a different color for each level or color code in your personal way.
- **Limit information to five to seven items on one branch.** The STM is limited in its capacity, and learning no more than seven items at a time will make it easier to get the information stored into your LTM.
- **Use one hierarchy for each chapter.** If you can't fit all of the information on one page, tape two pieces of paper together. You want to be able to visualize the entire picture.
- **Create a large hierarchy and tape it to your wall.** Study it often. Use posterboard or blank newspaper. Newspaper offices as well as office supply and discount stores sell inexpensive rolls of blank paper. Students have come up with creative ways to use recycled materials, including using cut-up cardboard from boxes and brown paper bags.

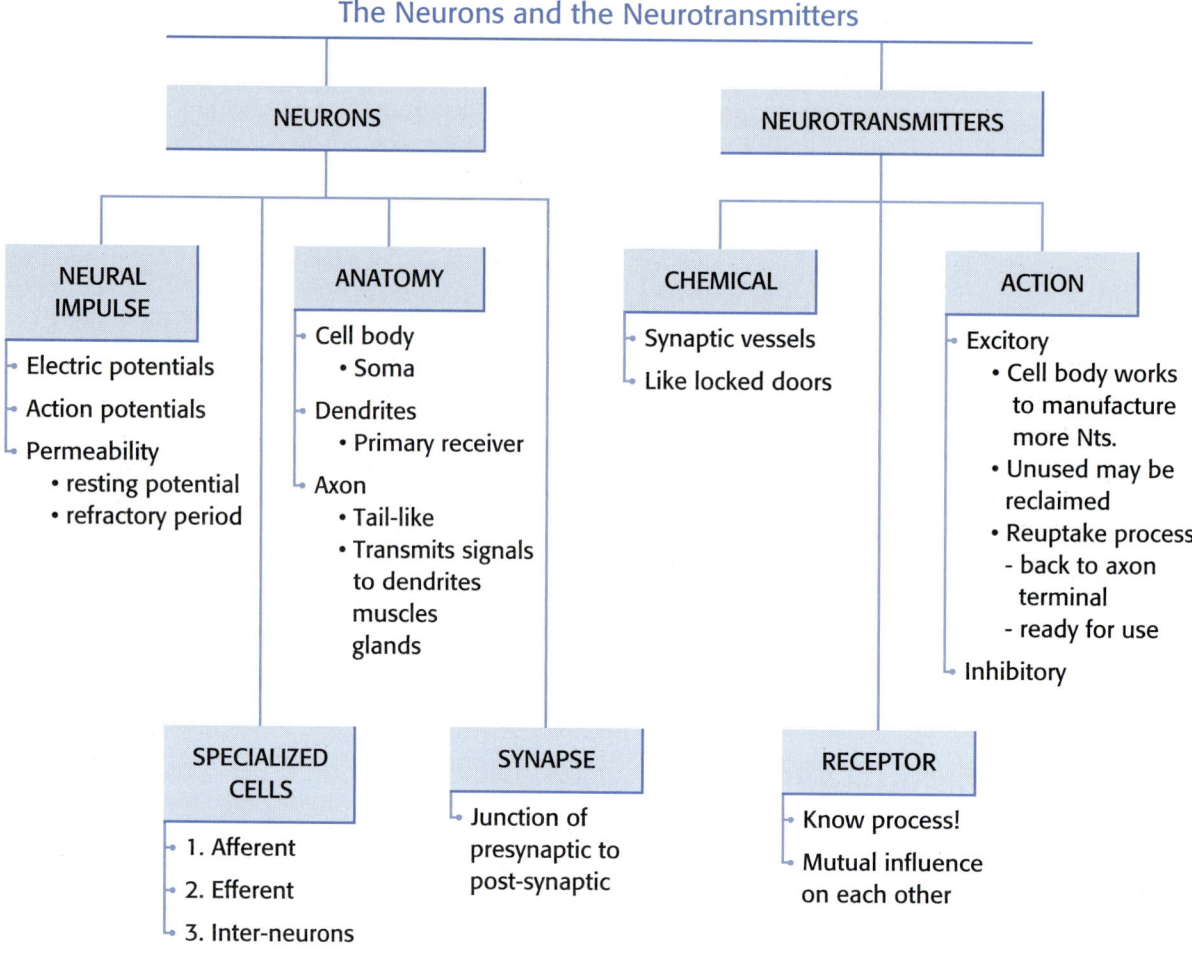

Figure 9.2 ■ Example of hierarchy.

Mind maps are similar to hierarchies in that they are a visual display of information. They can be used for notetaking, for generating ideas (brainstorming), or as a study tool. In mind mapping, symbols, colors, and pictures are used to enhance right-brain learning. It is a less structured form than the hierarchy. The main ideas are written in the center of the page, while the supporting details branch off in the direction you choose. A mind map allows you to bypass the linear, logical, critical left side of the brain, which can inhibit your creativity. Traditional notetaking is a left-brain process, while mind mapping gets processed on the right side. The little voice inside that says, "This is the wrong way to do it" or "This will never work," is quieted. Using mind-mapping techniques can feel awkward at first, but you may discover that it is a valuable missing piece of your learning process. It's also a great idea to use a mind map when you feel "stuck" or unmotivated. It gets you started.

Tips for creating mind maps:

- **Use different colors for main ideas and supporting details,** as you did in your hierarchy. When you study, close your eyes and see the map. This will enhance visual memory skills.
- **Draw as many pictures as you dare.** Remember that a picture is worth a thousand words. The right side of your brain holds this picture in your memory.
- **If you are using mind mapping to take class notes, add in textbook information.** If you are using mind mapping to take notes from your textbook, add class notes to it. Don't worry if it seems as though you are putting in an enormous effort. These techniques require more work in the beginning for a great payoff in the end. Figure 9.4 is an example of a mind map using the same information shown earlier from the psychology text.

THE NEURONS AND THE NEUROTRANSMITTERS

The Neurons: The Nervous System's Messenger Cells

All our thoughts, feelings, and behavior can ultimately be traced to the activity of **neurons**—the specialized cells that conduct impulses through the nervous system. Most experts estimate that there may be as many as 100 billion neurons in the brain (Swanson, 1995). This would mean that you have about 17 times as many neurons as there are people living on the earth right now.

Neurons perform several important tasks: (1) Afferent (sensory) neurons relay messages from the sense organs and receptors—eyes, ears, nose, mouth, and skin—to the brain or spinal cord. (2) Efferent (motor) neurons convey signals from the brain and spinal cord to the glands and the muscles, enabling the body to move. (3) Interneurons, thousands of times more numerous than motor or sensory neurons, carry information between neurons in the brain and between neurons in the spinal cord.

Anatomy of a Neuron: Looking at Its Parts   Although no two neurons are exactly alike, nearly all are made up of three important parts: the cell body (soma), dendrites, and the axon. The **cell body** contains the nucleus and carries out the metabolic, or life-sustaining, functions of the neuron. Branching out from the cell body are the **dendrites,** which look much like the leafless branches of a tree (*dendrite* comes from the Greek word for "tree"). The dendrites are the primary receivers of signals from other neurons, but the cell body can also receive signals directly. And dendrites do not merely receive signals from other neurons and relay them to the cell body. Scientists now know that dendrites relay messages backward—from the cell body to their own branches (a process called *back propagating*). These backward messages may shape the dendrites' responses to future signals they receive (Magee & Johnston, 1997; Sejnowski, 1997).

The **axon** is the slender, tail-like extension of the neuron that sprouts into many branches, each ending in a bulbous axon terminal. The axon terminals transmit signals to the dendrites or cell bodies of other neu-

Figure 2.1

The Structure of a Typical Neuron

A typical neuron has three important parts: (1) a cell body, which carries out the metabolic functions of the neuron; (2) branched fibers called dendrites, which are the primary receivers of the impulses from other neurons; and (3) a slender, tail-like extension called an axon, the transmitting end of the neuron, which sprouts into many branches, each ending in an axon terminal. The photograph shows human neurons greatly magnified.

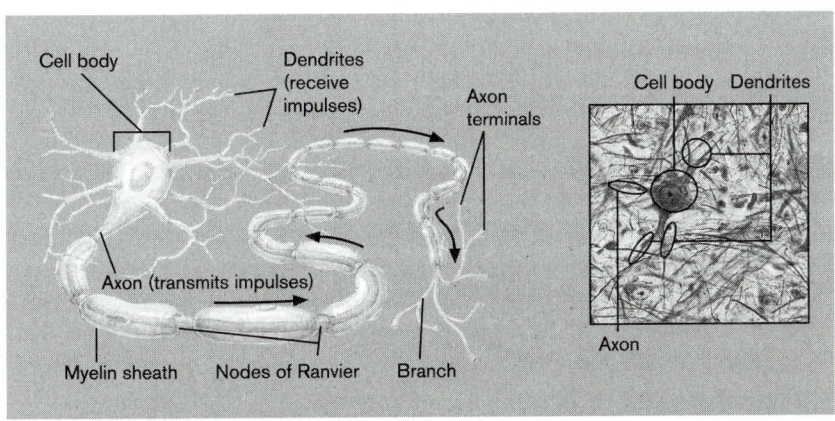

Figure 9.3 Pages from a college psychology textbook.

(*Source:* From Ellen R. Greenwood and Samuel E. Wood. *The World of Psychology,* 4th ed. Published by Allyn and Bacon, Boston, MA. Copyright © 2002 by Pearson Education. Reprinted by permission of the publisher.)

(*continued*)

rons, and to muscles, glands, and other parts of the body. In humans, some axons are short—only thousandths of an inch. Others can be up to a meter long—39.37 inches—long enough to reach from the brain to the tip of the spinal cord, or from the spinal cord to remote parts of the body. Figure 2.1 shows a neuron's structure.

The Synapse   Remarkably, the billions of neurons that send and receive signals are not physically connected. The axon terminals are separated from the receiving neurons by tiny, fluid-filled gaps called *synaptic clefts.* The **synapse** is the junction where the axon terminal of a sending (presynaptic) neuron communicates with a receiving (postsynaptic) neuron across the synaptic cleft. There may be as many as 100 trillion synapses in the human nervous system (Swanson, 1995). And a single neuron may synapse with thousands of other neurons (Kelner, 1997). A technique that has recently been developed to monitor the action at the synapses may soon enable researchers to visualize the activity of all the synapses of a single neuron.

If neurons are not physically connected, how do they communicate? How do they send and receive their messages?

The Neural Impulse: The Beginning of Thought and Action
Researchers have known for some 200 years that cells in the brain, the spinal cord, and the muscles generate electrical potentials. These tiny electric charges play a part in all bodily functions. Every time you move a muscle, experience a sensation, or have a thought or a feeling, a small but measurable electrical impulse is present.

How does this biological electricity work? Even though the impulse that travels down the axon is electrical, the axon does not transmit it the way a wire conducts an electrical current. What actually moves through the axon is a change in the **permeability** of the cell membrane. This process allows ions (electrically charged atoms or molecules) to move into and out of the axon through ion channels in the membrane.

Body fluids contain ions, some with positive electrical charges and others with negative charges. Inside the axon, there are normally more negative than positive ions. When at rest (not firing), the axon membrane carries a negative electrical potential of about −70 millivolts (70 thousandths of a volt) relative to the fluid outside the cell. This slight negative charge is referred to as the neuron's **resting potential.**

When the excitatory effects on a neuron reach a certain threshold, ion channels begin to open in the cell membrane of the axon at the point closest to the cell body, allowing positive ions to flow into the axon. This inflow of positive ions causes the membrane potential to change abruptly, to a positive value of about +50 millivolts (Pinel, 2000). This sudden reversal of the resting potential, which lasts for about 1 millisecond (1 thousandth of a second), is the **action potential.** Then the ion channels admitting positive ions close, and other ion channels open, forcing some positive ions out of the axon. As a result, the original negative charge, or resting potential, is restored. The opening and closing of ion channels continues segment by segment down the length of the axon, causing the action potential to move along the axon (Cardoso & Sabbatini, 2000).

The action potential operates according to the "all or none" law—a neuron either fires completely or does not fire at all. Immediately after a neuron fires, it enters a *refractory period,* during which it cannot fire again for 1 to 2 milliseconds. But this rest period is often very short: When stimulated, neurons can fire up to 1,000 times per second.

Figure 9.3

(continued)

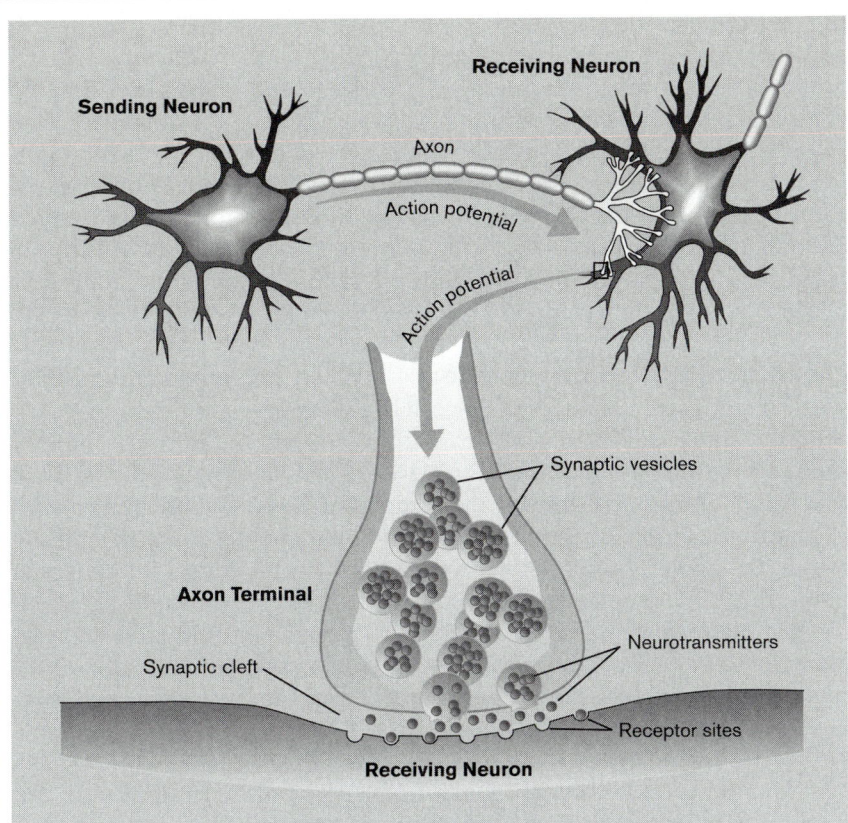

Figure 2.2
Synaptic Transmission

Sending neurons transmit their messages to receiving neurons by electrochemical action. When a neuron fires, the action potential arrives at the axon terminal and triggers the release of neurotransmitters from the synaptic vesicles. Neurotransmitters flow into the synaptic cleft and move toward the receiving neuron, which has numerous receptors. The receptors will bind only with neurotransmitters having distinctive molecular shapes that match their enclosed volumes. Neurotransmitters influence the receiving neuron only to fire or not to fire.

Neurotransmitters: The Chemical Messengers of the Brain

Once a neuron fires, how does it get its message across the synaptic cleft and on to other neurons? Messages are transmitted between neurons by one or more of a large group of chemical substances known as **neurotransmitters.**

Where are the neurotransmitters located? Inside the axon terminal are many small, sphere-shaped containers with thin membranes called *synaptic vesicles,* which hold the neurotransmitters. (*Vesicle* comes from a Latin word meaning "little bladder.") When an action potential arrives at the axon terminal, synaptic vesicles move toward the cell membrane, fuse with it, and release their neurotransmitter molecules. This process is shown in Figure 2.2.

The Receptor: Locks for Neurotransmitter Keys   Once released, neurotransmitters do not simply flow into the synaptic cleft and stimulate all the adjacent neurons. Each neurotransmitter has a distinctive molecular shape, and **receptors** on the surfaces of dendrites and cell bodies also have distinctive shapes. Neurotransmitters can affect only those neurons that have receptors designed to receive molecules of their particular shape. In other words, each receptor is somewhat like a locked door that only certain neurotransmitter keys can unlock (Cardoso & Sabbatini, 2000; Restak, 1993).

However, the binding of neurotransmitters with receptors is not as fixed and rigid a process as keys fitting locks or jigsaw puzzle pieces interlocking. Receptors in the brain are living matter; they can expand and contract their enclosed volumes. Consequently, the interaction where

Figure 9.3

(continued)

the neurotransmitter and the receptor meet is controlled not by the direct influence of one on the other, but by their *mutual* influence on each other. In such a dynamic interplay, a certain neurotransmitter may be competing for the same receptor with another neurotransmitter of a slightly different shape. The receptor will admit only one of the competing neurotransmitters—the one that fits it most perfectly. Thus, a receptor may receive a neurotransmitter at one time, but not at other times if another neurotransmitter molecule is present whose "affinity with the receptor is even stronger. As in dating and mating, what is finally settled for is always a function of what is available" (Restak, 1993, p. 28).

The Action of Neurotransmitters When neurotransmitters bind with receptors on the dendrites or cell bodies of receiving neurons, their action is either excitatory (influencing the neurons to fire) or inhibitory (influencing them not to fire). Because a single neuron may synapse with thousands of other neurons at the same time, there will always be both excitatory and inhibitory influences on receiving neurons. For the neuron to fire, the excitatory influences must exceed the inhibitory influences of neurotransmitter substances by a sufficient amount (the threshold).

For many years researchers believed that each individual neuron responded to only one neurotransmitter. But it is now known that individual neurons may respond to several different neurotransmitters, suggesting a greater flexibility of response, even at the level of a single neuron (Pinel, 2000).

You may wonder how the synaptic vesicles can continue to pour out neurotransmitters, yet have a ready supply so that the neuron can respond to continuing stimulation. First, the cell body of the neuron is always working to manufacture more of the neurotransmitter substance. Second, unused neurotransmitters in the synaptic cleft may be broken down into their component molecules and reclaimed by the axon terminal to be recycled and used again. Third, by an important process called **reuptake,** the neurotransmitter substance is taken back into the axon terminal, intact and ready for immediate use. This terminates the neurotransmitter's excitatory or inhibitory effect on the receiving neuron. Figure 2.3 illustrates the reuptake process.

The nature of synaptic transmission—whether it is primarily chemical or electrical—was a subject of controversy during the first half of the 20th century. By the 1950s, it seemed clear that the means of communication between neurons was chemical. Yet, at some synapses, what was termed "gap junction," or electrical transmission, occurred between the neurons. Recent research has shown that this electrical transmission may be more frequent than neuroscientists once believed (Bennett, 2000). Even though synaptic transmission of information between neurons is primarily chemical, some electrical transmission is known to occur at synapses in the retina, the olfactory bulb (sense of smell), and the cerebral cortex, which we will discuss later in the chapter (Bennett, 2000).

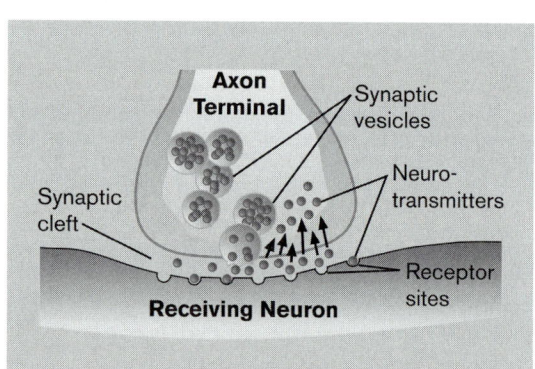

Figure 2.3

The Process of Reuptake

Through the process of reuptake, neurotransmitter molecules are taken back into the axon terminal, intact and ready for immediate use.

Figure 9.3

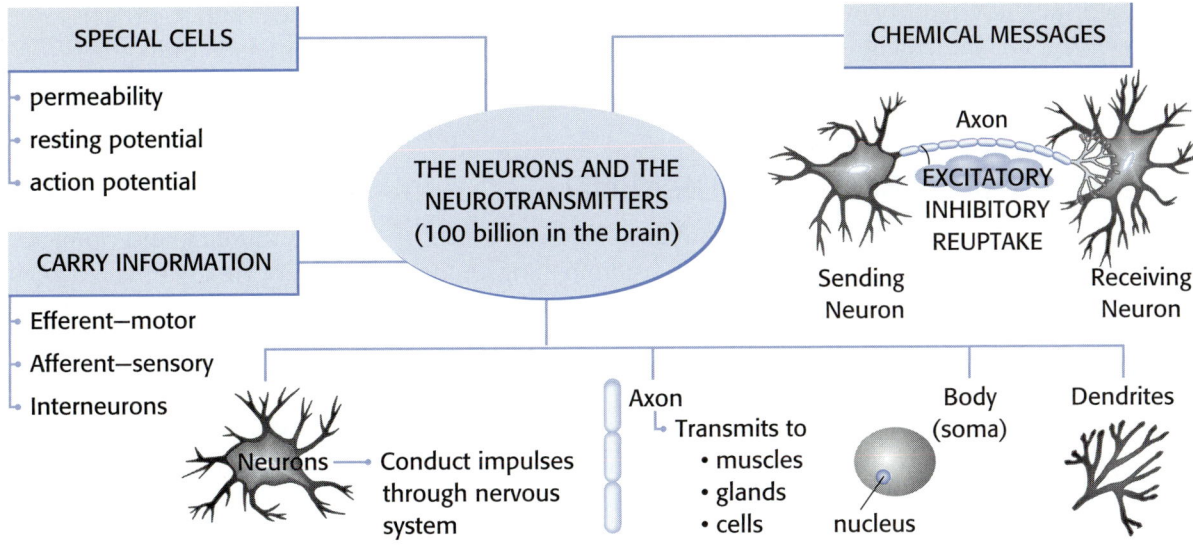

Figure 9.4 ■ Mind map.

DEVELOPING YOUR PHOTOGRAPHIC MEMORY

A photographic memory is the ability to read or view something once and fully remember it. Only a small segment of the population has this gift, but everyone can increase their visual or photographic memory. Your visual memory is working all of the time. For example, think of pictures, sayings, or magnets that you have on your refrigerator door. If you close your eyes, you will most likely be able to remember what's on it. That is because every time you go to your refrigerator, your visual memory (right brain) is taking a picture of it. These pictures get stored without your conscious awareness. Think of what you could remember if you practiced using your photographic right brain. The following exercises will help you develop this skill.

- **Choose an ordinary object and look carefully at it.** Notice *everything* you can about it, including shape, color, texture, and size. When you feel ready, look away from it and view it with your eyes closed. Does the picture in your mind look like the "real" object? Keep practicing until you see the exact picture. Once you master simple objects, you can move on to more complicated pictures.
- When you are reading a short story or novel, create a movie of it in your mind. See the characters and watch the action.
- *Study Tip*: Close your eyes and visualize yourself taking an upcoming exam. Take a few deep breaths and relax. Imagine that the instructor is passing out the exam. Now visualize yourself answering the questions correctly and happily handing in your paper. *Mental rehearsal* builds photographic images. Feel your success.
- **Do what the athletes do.** Did you know that visualizing is part of an athlete's training? Have you ever watched an Olympic figure skater before a performance? As she waits patiently to go on the ice, she stands still with her eyes closed while her head is moving and bobbing around. She is imagining a perfect performance. This picture and feeling of success are imprinted on the visual (right) side of the brain. Because visualization techniques work, they are an important part of sports psychology.
- **As you read textbooks, begin making color pictures of the information in your mind.** For example, if you are reading about stem cell research in a biology text, visualize the process by which the cells create new cells. Create a video of it in your mind. Add music. Make the cells

colorful and watch them change. Use your imagination. This is a complex skill, so do not worry if it is difficult at first. The way to develop your photographic mind is to think in pictures.

TRICKING THE SUBCONSCIOUS MIND

The conscious mind is the part of your mind that you are aware of; it is the thinking and problem-solving part, the one that busies itself with decision making and "mind chatter." At any time, you can know what you are thinking. Your subconscious, on the other hand, is the part of the mind that you are not aware of, yet it plays an important role in your life; it motivates everything you do, and that makes it powerful! Here's an example of how your mind works:

> You are driving in your car, and realize that soon you will need to make a left-hand turn. You *consciously* turn your left signal on and execute the turn. You're driving along and soon you are pulling into your driveway, but you don't remember driving there. Your thoughts were somewhere else. You were thinking about your vacation, or your last date, or remembering what you need to pick up at the grocery store. Your conscious mind was free to drift off, while your subconscious mind became more active and got you home. When you realize that you're home, your awareness shifts and your conscious mind takes over.

Self-Talk is speaking directly to your subconscious mind, which takes in information and processes it literally. In other words, it believes whatever you tell it. Talking to the subconscious mind is like talking to a 6-year-old child. Think of a time when you have called someone, and a young child answers the phone. You ask politely, "Is your mother home?" You hear a resounding yes and then you hear nothing. The phone hasn't gone dead; your question has been answered with a one-word answer, and the child has responded quite literally. If an adult had answered the phone, the response might have been different: "Yeah, she's here—wait just a minute and I'll get her."

Because the subconscious mind believes what we tell it, it's vital to be positive when we talk to ourselves. Our minds are active and busy. We're always thinking. What do you say when you talk to yourself?

Understanding how the subconscious works can help create a positive learning environment. There will be occasions when you'll have to take a class that is not your first choice. Perhaps the class meets too early, or you don't like the way the instructor lectures. The trick is turning a negative situation into a positive one by using the power of your mind. You do it by PRETENDING. Tell yourself that the instructor is the most dynamic you've ever had, that the material is simply fascinating, that this is the most interesting class you've ever attended. Get the idea? You're tricking your subconscious. Remember that it is taking in information literally, and it believes what you tell it. If you are enjoying your experience, you'll learn more. There is power in self-affirmation. Use what you know about the subconscious mind to your advantage.

ACTIVITIES

Activity 1: Creating a Hierarchy

Directions: Using a textbook from one of your classes, create a hierarchy for one chapter. With a partner or in a small group, test yourself on the material using only your hierarchy. How did it work? Share your responses.

Activity 2: Creating a Mind Map

Directions: Using the same material that you used to do a hierarchy, create a mind map.

Activity 3: Converting from Right Brain to Left Brain

Directions: Convert the information from your mind map or hierarchy into a summary. Remember that a summary is a condensed version of the text material, highlighting the main points.

Activity 4: Developing Visual Memory

Directions: Choose an object to view. Look at it for several minutes, and then look away from it. Close your eyes and try to picture the object. Next, open your eyes and look at it from different angles. Close your eyes and picture it. With your eyes closed, pretend you have a zoom lens and zoom into the picture. Zoom back out. Now look at it as if you were standing above it. Next, look at it as if you were standing below it. Open your eyes and look at the object for about ten seconds. Close your eyes and see its colors and textures. Open your eyes. At some time during the day, close your eyes and see if you can remember the object in detail.

CHAPTER 10
Active Listening and Notetaking

I think the one lesson I have learned is that there is no substitute for paying attention.

—Diane Sawyer, journalist

ACTIVE LISTENING: A GREAT BEGINNING!

Successful notetaking requires the ability to listen. If you ask someone if he considers himself a good listener, you'd probably get a "yes" response. The truth is that people don't always listen well. We might hear the words that someone is speaking, but we don't always pay attention to the meaning. Our thoughts drift to our own concerns, we may "tune out" and come back to the conversation, or even be accused of not listening. Clearly, there is a difference between hearing and listening. This can happen during class as well. Many students sit in class and take notes on the instructor's lecture, only to realize that they've been "somewhere else" for awhile. They quickly realize that they've missed some important points. They now know that they haven't really been paying attention, even though they've heard the instructor's voice. Remember that what you pay attention to is also what you miss!

Successful notetaking requires active listening. *Active listening* means listening with awareness and intent. It is listening to understand the lecture and to think about what is being said. Every instructor has her own organizational pattern for giving a lecture, and it's your job to discover it. It will assist you in taking good class notes.

Generally, a lecture will begin with a main topic followed by supporting information, which expands and explains the main idea. When you are listening actively, you are getting the whole picture. At first, it might seem difficult to listen and take notes at the same time, but ongoing practice will make it easier to do. *Active listening* and successful notetaking are skills that can be developed.

Tips for becoming an active listener:

- **Sit as close to the instructor as you dare.** Remember this tip from Chapter 8 on concentration, and keep your eyes on the speaker. It will help you keep distractions to a minimum.
- **Listen for main ideas** and think about how the supporting details fit for each one.
- **Be alert.** Recognize when a new idea is being introduced.

- **Keep an open mind.** Becoming emotionally upset or angry will not work to your advantage. Keep taking notes. If you find yourself in disagreement with the instructor, make an appointment to talk with him during his office hours. Be honest with your instructor, and let him know your feelings.
- **Aim for excellent concentration.** Engage in self-talk. Tell yourself that you are "getting" all of the information.
- **Test your *active listening* skills.** Practice with a friend. When you are engaged in conversation, listen actively and don't talk for awhile. You may be surprised at the outcome.
- **Be sure that you've had enough sleep the night before class.** It's difficult to listen and take good notes when you are tired.
- **Don't come to class hungry.** Low blood sugar can affect your ability to concentrate.
- If you are bored in class, **add your own ideas to your notes.** Think about the material you are learning.

Listen for *cue words* that move the lecture along. Your instructor is constantly giving you hints to help you take good notes. Listen for cue words and you will be able to follow the direction of the lecture, as well as discover which ideas the instructor thinks are important. *Here are some examples:*

- Cue words for *Examples*: For example, for instance, to illustrate
- Cue words for *Organization* or *Steps in Order*: The six steps are . . ., next, finally, first, second, third
- Cue words for *additional points*: Furthermore, in addition, also, moreover
- Cue words for *opposing ideas*: On the other hand, in contrast, although, however
- Cue words for *similar ideas*: Likewise, similarly, to compare
- Cue words for *exceptions*: However, nevertheless, but, yet, still
- Cue words for *emphasis*: Above all, finally, more important
- Cue words for *understanding*: In other words, in essence, briefly
- Cue words for *summarizing*: In conclusion, to sum up, for these reasons, in a nutshell
- Cue words for *exams*: Remember this, this is important, this could be on the test

Pay attention to these words and phrases when you are reading your texts, as well as when you are listening to take notes.

PREPARATION FOR EXCELLENT NOTETAKING

It is a myth that sitting in class and just listening will earn you good grades. Taking class notes is necessary for learning and remembering. Remember that the short-term memory doesn't store information; taking notes will help you make the transfer into the long-term memory. It can also help you concentrate and focus on material in the lecture.

Tips for preparing to take notes:

- **Have homework assignments read** before you come to class and take notes. It is always easier to learn material when it is familiar. Keep current with your reading assignments.
- **Have all of your supplies ready to use.** Open your notebook to a blank page or have your laptop ready to go. Bring colored pens or pencils to class for notetaking. You can miss important information when you go digging into your purse or backpack to look for a pen.
- **Don't let yourself feel overwhelmed by the notetaking process.** Practice is required for improvement. Over time, it will become easier. Do breathing or visualization exercises before each class session. Use positive self-talk and affirmations.
- **Arrive to class early** and get a good seat away from distractions. Could these distractions be your friends?
- **Remember to use active listening skills.**

TAKING NOTES

Excellent notetaking consists of (1) active listening, (2) focused attention, and (3) the intention to understand. Here are some valuable tips for taking notes:

- **Come to class mentally prepared** to take notes for the entire period.
- **Begin to take notes** as soon as the instructor begins lecturing. Don't wait until you think you've heard an important idea. Everything is important!
- **Write down key words, main ideas, and supporting details.** Keep in mind that exams are comprehensive. You will not have sufficient information if you only write down main ideas. Write down explanations, facts, terms, and definitions.
- **Pay attention to cue words.** Memorize the list of cue words in this chapter.
- **Write down everything that your instructor writes on the board.** If it's important enough for her to write it, it's important enough to be on a test.
- **Write down everything that is emphasized on an overhead projector.** This is possible test exam material.
- **When revising your notes, color-code them.** Use a different color pen for main ideas, supporting details, or examples. For example, use yellow for main ideas, blue for supporting details, and pink for examples.
- **Take notes in the instructor's words**, but when you study, recite them in **your own words to** *personalize* the information.
- **Leave blank spaces** if you can't get all of the information down. You can fill the page later with notes from another student. Ask your instructor for a copy of her notes. Check your textbooks, too.
- **Leave white space** between the main ideas and the supporting details. This will help you determine the organization of the lecture.
- **Pay attention to your instructor's style of lecturing.** Some instructors are organized and easy to follow, while others may quickly switch topics or tell a story before getting back to the original point. If you need to, leave room in your notes and catch up later. Discovering your instructor's lecturing style will help you make adjustments in your notetaking.
- **Check to see** whether the instructor's lecture comes directly from the textbook. If the lecture does come straight from the text, you can refer to the book and add necessary or additional information to your class notes. If the lecture material is not from the text, take notes from your book and compare them to the information in the lecture.
- **Take notes until the end of the class period,** even if everyone else is getting ready to leave. An instructor wants to make sure that all of the material is presented, and an important idea can come at the very end of class. If you're packing up your books, you can easily miss the information.
- **Remember that your notetaking skills improve with practice.** Practice at home by taking notes from a TV documentary, DVD, or videotape. Use material that is organized and instructional.
- **Pay attention to the instructor's "pet" or favorite ideas.** Any ideas that an instructor finds worth repeating are important enough to be on a test.
- **Write legibly.** You can't learn from your notes if you can't read them. It's OK to write in phrases when you take notes, but you need to be able to understand what you've written. If you can't, then try writing in complete sentences.
- **Use an adjusted writing style.** This style combines cursive writing and printing. It allows you to write rapidly in a style that is legible. See Figure 10.1.

Enid Leonard	cursive
Enid Leonard	printing
Enid Leonard	adjusted

Figure 10.1 ■ Styles of writing.

- **Use a tape recorder in class** if you are still having trouble taking notes; however, it is generally not recommended. Becoming dependent on a tape recorder won't build your confidence for in-class notetaking. It certainly can be useful if you are an auditory learner, a commuter, or a non-native speaker. If you know that you're going to be absent from class, you can have someone tape the lecture for you (with permission from the instructor). The ideal is to take your own excellent notes. (See Figure 10.2.)

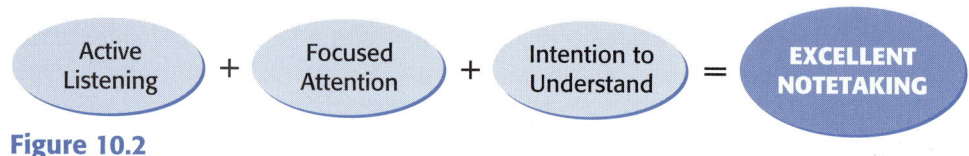

Figure 10.2

ESTABLISHING YOUR CONSISTENT SYSTEM

Consistency is a vital component of efficient notetaking. It means taking notes the same way each time. Having a consistent system allows you to understand your notes. Once you have established a pattern for notetaking that works, don't change it. One student looked at her notes years after having a class and was amazed at how clear and understandable they were.

Tips for creating a consistent notetaking system:

- **Develop your own shorthand method.** Use symbols and abbreviations as much as possible. Once you've established a symbol for something, use it consistently.
- **Shorten words by omitting vowels.** This is the same concept used in creating designer car license plates.

  Prblm—problem   bkgd—background   histry—history   vwl—vowel

- Use standard abbreviations in place of words.

  w—with   w/o—without   b4—before   + or &—and
  =—equals   %—percent   c—with   ∴—therefore

- **Use the first part of a word for the full word.**

  info—information   psych—psychology   est—estimate   symb—symbolic

- **Create your own symbols.** For example, if you are taking a Sociology class, you could use:

  soc—sociology /sociological   O—family   soc-N—social norms
  S.Inst—social institutions   SD—social density (K)—kinship

  For general notetaking, use:

  B.C—because   (m)—most importantly   c→—compared to   Ex—example

- **Add symbols, pictures, and drawings to your notes** as you review. Make them different sizes and colors. This is a great right-brain activity.

Write notes to yourself.
Example: *See page 47 of text on notes from date . . .*

SHORT CUTS FOR STRESSFUL TIMES

Stress can affect your ability to take complete notes. Here are some suggestions for those days when you're not "up to speed."

- **Take the best notes** that you can under stressful conditions. Ask a student in class if you can look at his or her notes. Establishing a relationship with another student can be mutually beneficial. Exchange phone numbers.
- **If you know you will not be attending class,** call a friend and ask her to make copies of her notes. When you return to class, ask the instructor if he has any additional information for you.
- **If you are suffering emotional stress** and you feel that your concentration is too poor to take notes, ask the instructor if you may tape the lecture. Later, take notes from the tape in a less stressful environment. The important thing is to always have class notes, whether you take them yourself or get them from someone else.
- **See a drop-in counselor at your school.** Don't put off getting help. Try to keep up with your assignments. Study someone else's notes.
- **Sit in a different seat.** Create a new association for learning.
- **Ask questions**; it will keep you alert in class.

THE CORNELL NOTETAKING SYSTEM

Many different notetaking systems have been developed through the years. Choosing one that fits your learning style will build confidence in your ability. Knowing different systems can provide flexibility. The instructor's style of lecturing may be a consideration when choosing a preferred style.

The Cornell System was developed at Cornell University more than 40 years ago and continues to be popular with college students. Here are the guidelines for taking Cornell notes:

- Take notes on one side of the page only.
- Draw a 2 ½ inch margin down the left side of the page. This is called the cue column. College bookstores often sell notetaking paper with the margin already printed on each page. Check your campus bookstore or art supply shop. You may also leave several inches of space on the bottom of each page for writing a summary. Some students prefer to have a separate page for summarizing their notes after each class session.
- Include the date and class name on each page. You may include the instructor's name and the time of the class.

Steps in the Cornell Notetaking System

1. Take notes on the right side of the paper only. Remember to leave the 2 ½ inch margin blank. You will fill that in at a later time. Be as comprehensive as possible in getting the information from the lecture.
2. *After* the lecture, while the information is still fresh in your mind, use the cue column to write study questions, key words, or phrases that are related to the notes that you took on the right side of the page. You will use these as cues to test yourself on the material in your notes. Filling in the cue column while you are taking notes defeats the system. When you have completed the cue column, you are ready for the next step.
3. Cover up the notes on the right side of the page and use the cue column to test your knowledge of the material. Use the key words and phrases to help you remember the main ideas and supporting information from the lecture. If you wrote study questions, try to answer them. Recite out loud and in your own words. If you cannot answer your questions or do not know the material at this point, go back and study your notes and begin the process again. This important step will provide feedback for you. It lets you know if you're learning and understanding the material.
4. Write a summary of the information on the bottom of each page or use one sheet for each notetaking session. A summary clarifies the main ideas for you.
5. Review your notes immediately and continue with regular review periods. Reviewing your notes on a daily basis helps store the information into your long-term memory.
6. Study the information using flash cards, outlines, hierarchies, and mind maps. Think about the material and make connections to what you already know. Remember what you learned in

Chapter 9 on memory. This step involves integrating the material, so you can understand it at a deep level. You're not just memorizing it, you know it.

An example of the Cornell Notetaking System is shown in Figure 10.3.

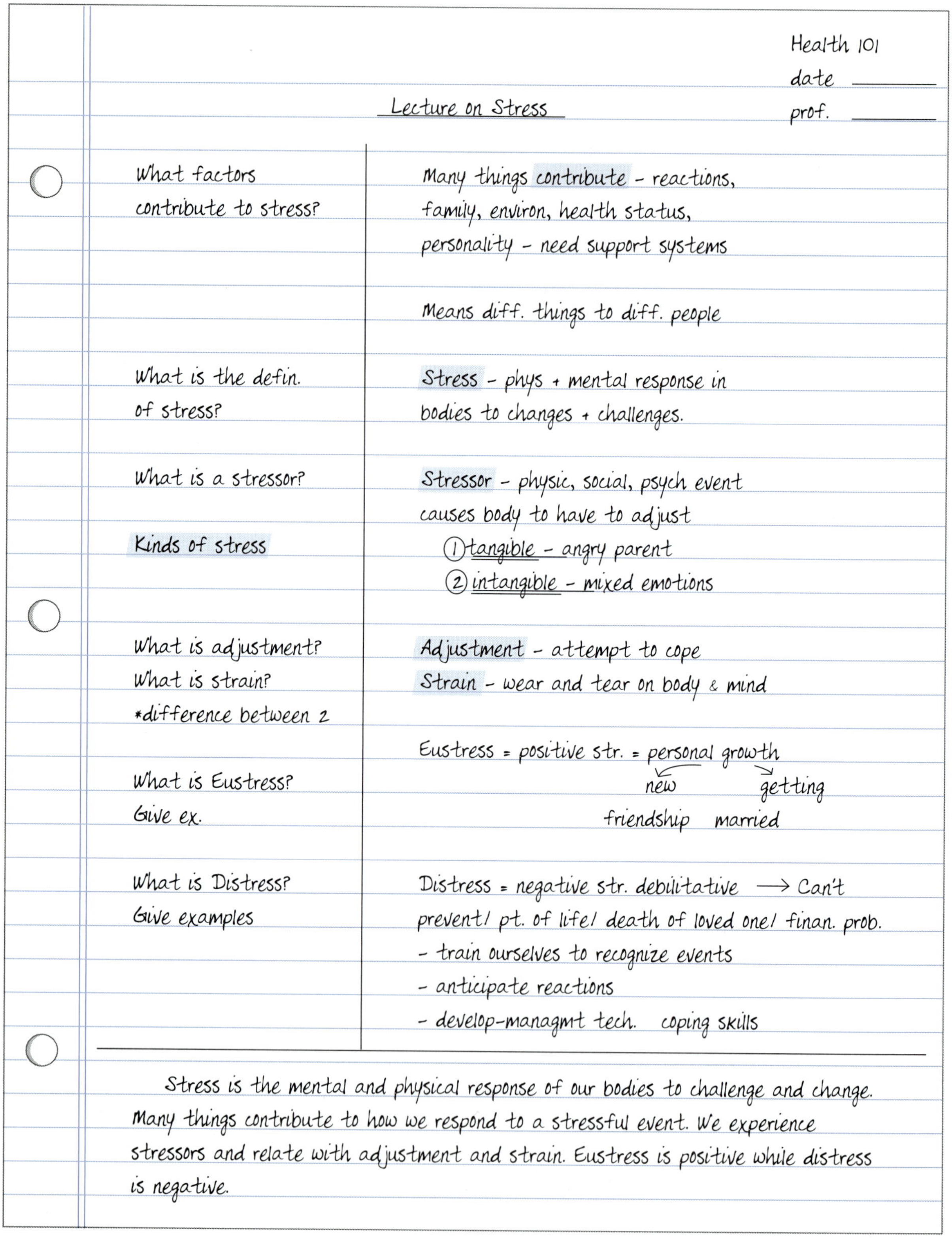

Health 101
date _____
prof. _____

Lecture on Stress

What factors contribute to stress?	Many things contribute - reactions, family, environ, health status, personality - need support systems
	Means diff. things to diff. people
What is the defin. of stress?	Stress - phys + mental response in bodies to changes + challenges.
What is a stressor?	Stressor - physic, social, psych event causes body to have to adjust
Kinds of stress	① tangible - angry parent ② intangible - mixed emotions
What is adjustment? What is strain? *difference between 2	Adjustment - attempt to cope Strain - wear and tear on body & mind

What is Eustress?
Give ex.
	Eustress = positive str. = personal growth
	    new getting
	  friendship married

What is Distress? Give examples	Distress = negative str. debilitative → Can't prevent/ pt. of life/ death of loved one/ finan. prob. - train ourselves to recognize events - anticipate reactions - develop-managmt tech. coping skills

Stress is the mental and physical response of our bodies to challenge and change. Many things contribute to how we respond to a stressful event. We experience stressors and relate with adjustment and strain. Eustress is positive while distress is negative.

Figure 10.3 Cornell Notetaking System

THE LEONARD NOTETAKING SYSTEM

The Leonard System combines notetaking with study flash cards. Notes are taken on 5 × 7-inch cards. It is preferable to use the spiral-bound cards, which are easy to carry in your backpack or notebook. They keep your notes organized and in one place. Before you begin taking notes, write your name, the instructor's name, and the name and time of your class on the front flap cover. If your note cards get lost, they can be returned to you.

Steps in the Leonard Notetaking System

1. Take notes on one side of the card. You may want to leave a few cards blank to add information from your textbook or handouts at a later time.
2. Turn the card over and write study questions and key words that are related to the material on the front side. Add symbols and pictures to incorporate right-brain learning. Color code as previously suggested. One idea is to use one color for class notes and a different color for study questions and symbols.
3. Use the questions, symbols, and pictures on the back of each card to test yourself on the material. Use it as a flash card. If you can't answer a question, put the card in a separate stack and ask the question again later. Keep testing yourself until there are no cards stacked.

Figures 10.4 and 10.5 show examples of the Leonard system of notetaking.

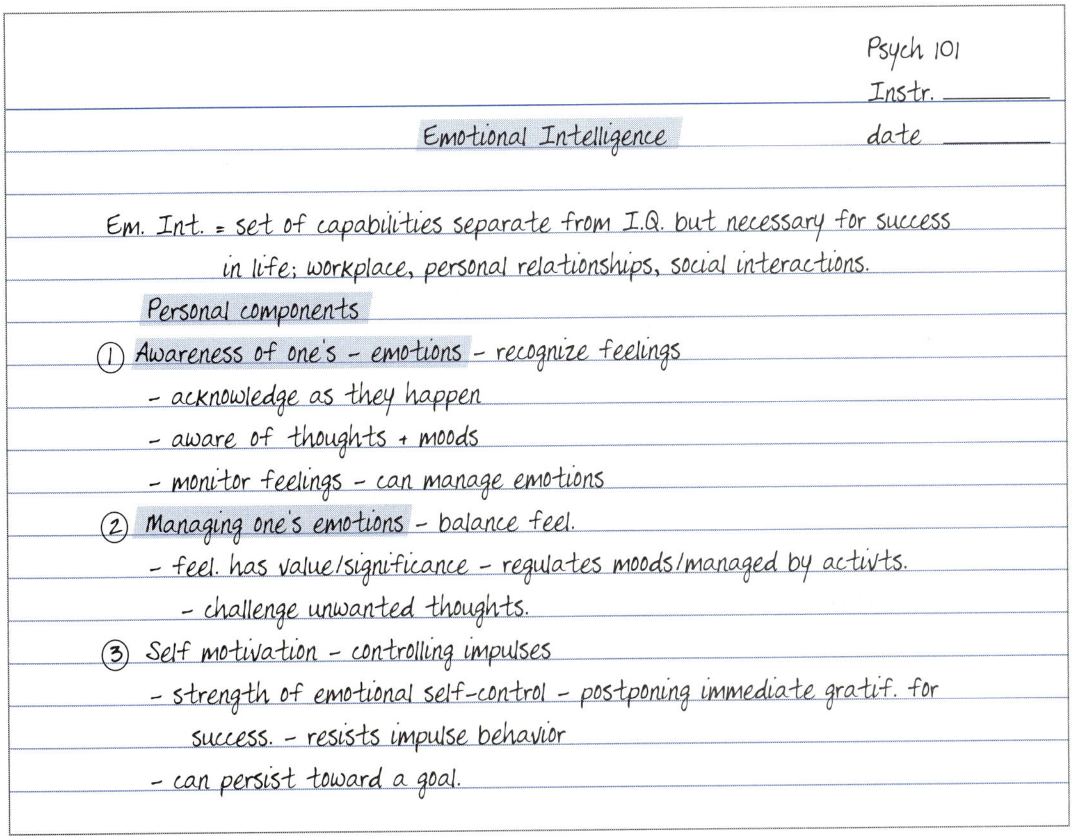

Figure 10.4 Example of Leonard system of notetaking.

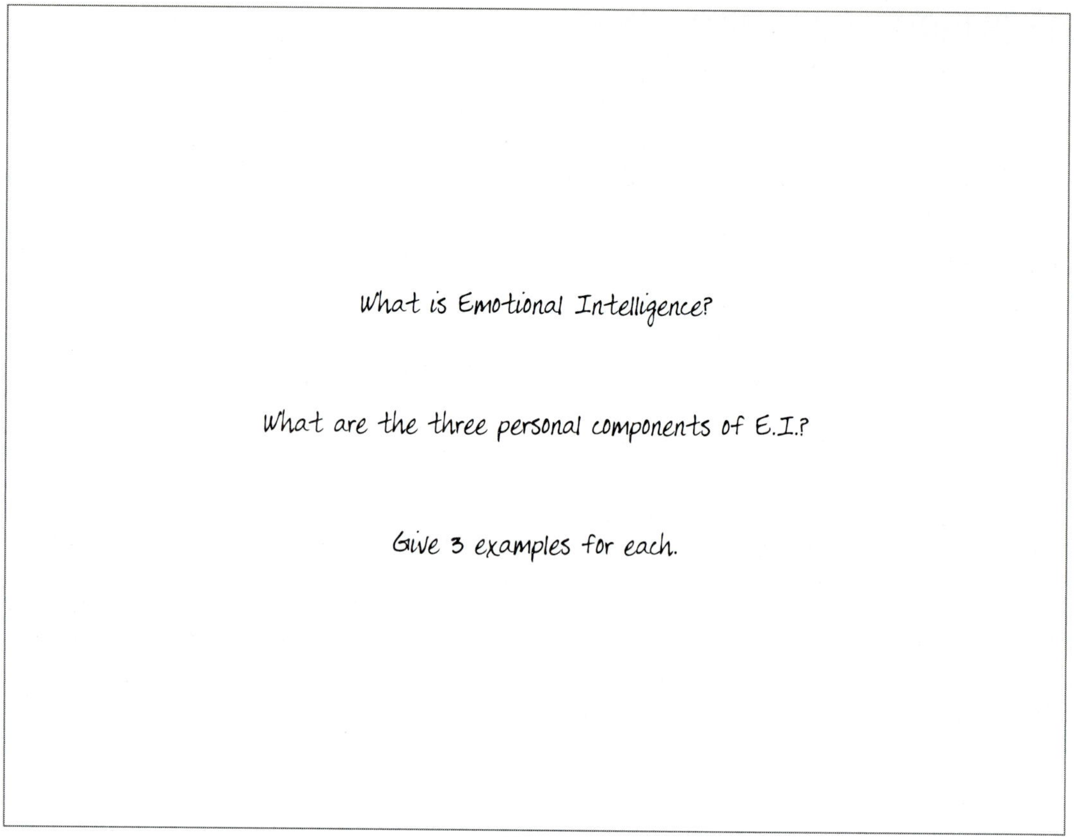

> What is Emotional Intelligence?
>
> What are the three personal components of E.I.?
>
> Give 3 examples for each.

Figure 10.5 Another example of Leonard system of notetaking.

ACTIVITIES

Activity 1: Listening and Communication Exercise

Directions: Bring a pen-and-ink drawing or picture to class. Work in partners for this exercise. One person will describe the picture as accurately as possible for the other person to draw. The person giving the oral directions may answer questions but may not show the drawing to the "artist." When the drawing is complete, compare it to the original. What's different? What is the same? How did giving directions affect the outcome? Discuss your listening and communication styles.

Activity 2: Notetaking Practice

Directions: Choose a documentary video and take notes from it. Use the Cornell or Leonard System. When you've completed taking notes, replay the video and check your accuracy. Write a summary.

Activity 3: Guest Lecturer

Directions: Have your instructor bring in a guest lecturer to present a 20- or 25-minute talk. Take notes, and then have the guest speaker pass out a set of her notes. Compare your notes to hers by putting an * (asterisk) next to the information that matches.

CHAPTER 11
Textbooks: Reading, Highlighting, and Notetaking

Tell me, and I'll forget. Show me, and I may remember.
Involve me, and I'll understand.

—Author unknown

READING TEXTBOOKS

Reading a college textbook requires different reading skills than the ones used to read a novel or magazine. Textbooks are packed with information. Ideas are discussed in great detail, and serious attention is required to learn the information that is presented. The best way to master textbook material is to begin with the initial step of *previewing* or *surveying*. You may notice that this skill has been presented in other chapters. That's because organizing information is an essential part of learning and studying. Before you tackle your first reading assignment, survey the entire text. Begin by learning what you can from the

1. Title Page
2. Table of Contents
3. Preface or Introduction to the Student
4. Glossary—an alphabetical list of terms
5. Index—subjects in alphabetical order at the back of the book. This is an excellent tool for finding information quickly.
6. Appendix—supplemental material at the back of the text. In this book, the Appendix has time management and calendar forms for you to use.

The task of reading text material can be overwhelming, and as if that isn't enough, there's an exam covering every chapter. Using a multi-step reading system will assist you in mastering textbook material. One such time-honored system is SQ3R, which stands for (1) Survey, (2) Question, (3) Read, (4) Recite, and (5) Review.

SQ3R

Step 1. **Survey.** Surveying or previewing gives you the "big picture." Before you delve into the chapter, spend a few minutes reading headings and subheadings, introductions and summaries. Look at pictures and graphs, and read study questions that follow the chapter. Make mental notes of vocabulary words. Will you need a dictionary to read this text? Surveying provides an overview that will help you become familiar with the material.

Step 2. **Question.** Turn chapter headings and subheadings into questions as you read. Your busy left brain (the language side) naturally wants to answer the question because it's the problem-solving part of the brain. This step helps you focus and identify main ideas. If there are no subheadings to guide you, turn the first sentence into a question. Write your questions in the margin of the text or in your notebook.

Step 3. **Read.** Read carefully, keeping your questions in mind. Underline the answers to the questions, main ideas, and important supporting details. Think about what you are reading and try to connect the new ideas to ones that you already know. How do the details support the main ideas? Write down ideas as you read. Become an active reader.

Step 4. **Recite.** "Talk the material." After reading a section, look away from the text and try to recite the material in your own words. You practiced this step in the Cornell and Leonard notetaking systems. Reciting helps you learn and store information in the long-term memory.

Step 5. **Review.** Begin reviewing immediately, and continue to review throughout the term. Write summaries of the information in the chapter. Some texts have questions at the end of a chapter for you to answer. Create flash cards, outlines, or mind maps. Use your time-management schedule to designate review and study periods.

Additional tips for reading texts:

- *Always* read with a pen or pencil in hand and be ready to mark important information. This technique uses hand-eye coordination (visual-kinesthetic modes) and helps you focus on the material. You are developing a positive pattern. Your subconscious knows that when you pick up a pen, you are ready for serious reading and comprehension.
- **Look for main ideas** that are often the first sentence of a paragraph. Pay attention to when a new idea begins.
- **Review often.** By now, you know that reviewing is an essential skill for learning and remembering. Studying textbook material is similar to studying class notes; they both require ongoing review. Spend time with your textbooks and notes. The payoff is worth the energy and time.
- **Read other sources related to the material.** You may be able to find a guidebook that can help you clarify the information. Do a Google search on the Internet to find related materials.
- **Pretend that you are having a discussion with the author.** Do you agree or disagree with his ideas? This process helps you become an active reader.
- Without looking, **recite the information** that you have in your summaries.
- If the material is difficult to understand, **read it out loud.** Hearing the material can help you understand it (auditory learning). Modulate your voice.

HIGHLIGHTING AND MARKING TEXTBOOKS

Textbook marking helps you sort out the organization of the material you are reading, so you can determine which ideas are important. When you know what to study, preparing for an exam becomes easier.

Tips for marking a text:

- *Preview* **before you begin marking the chapter** (Step 1 in SQ3R). Highlight main ideas, key concepts, numbered items, definitions, and examples. Use a yellow marker or color of your choice. Some students use several colors to separate main ideas from supporting information. When you highlight, *less is more.* Mark sparingly. Marking everything defeats the purpose.
- **Use brackets** [ ] { } to mark longer passages. It's efficient and easy on the eyes.
- **Circle key concepts** or put ☐'s around numbered items.
- **Mark up your textbooks.** Because reading is an active process rather than a passive one like watching TV, you need to be involved. When you're involved, you're learning. Don't be afraid to argue with the author by writing comments in the margin. Get involved. Use your right brain; get emotional and interact with the material. Develop your consistent marking system and you'll have a great study aid that you can always count on.
- **Write questions in the margin.** You can use it as a recall column to test yourself.

Figure 11.1(a) is an example of textbook highlighting and marking.

AIR POLLUTION

Although we often assume that the air we breathe is safe, the daily impact of a growing population makes clean air more difficult to find. Concern about air quality prompted Congress to pass the Clean Air Act in 1970 and to amend it in 1977 and again in 1990. The object was to develop standards for six of the most widespread air pollutants that seriously affect health: sulfur dioxide, particulates, carbon monoxide, nitrogen dioxide, ozone, and lead. Table 21.1 shows the number of Americans still living in counties where air standards are not met.

TABLE 21.1
Percent of Americans Living in U.S. Counties That Meet Air Quality Standards

All pollutants	75%
Ozone standards	80%
Carbon monoxide standards	94%
Particulates	95%
Sulfur dioxide standards	100%
Nitrogen dioxide standards	100%
Lead standards	98%

Source: Health, United States: 1996–97, U.S. National Center for Health Statistics, Washington, DC: USDHHS, Public Health Service.

Sources of Air Pollution

▸ *Sulfur Dioxide* **Sulfur dioxide** is a yellowish brown gas that is a by-product of burning fossil fuels. Electricity generating stations, smelters, refineries, and industrial boilers are the main source points. In humans, sulfur dioxide aggravates symptoms of heart and lung disease, obstructs breathing passages, and increases the incidence of respiratory diseases such as colds, asthma, bronchitis, and emphysema. It is toxic to plants, destroys some paint pigments, corrodes metals, impairs visibility, and is a precursor to acid rain, which we discuss later in this chapter.

▸ *Particulates* **Particulates** are tiny solid particles or liquid droplets that are suspended in the air. Cigarette smoke releases particulates. They are also by-products of some industrial processes and the internal combustion engine. Particulates can in and of themselves irritate the lungs and can additionally carry heavy metals and carcinogenic agents deep into the lungs. When combined with sulfur dioxide, they exacerbate respiratory diseases. Particulates can also corrode metals and obscure visibility. Numerous scientific studies have found significant links between exposure to air particulate concentrations at or below current standards and adverse health effects, including premature death.[11]

▸ *Carbon Monoxide* **Carbon monoxide** is an odorless, colorless gas that originates primarily from motor vehicle emissions. Carbon monoxide interferes with the blood's ability to absorb and carry oxygen and can impair thinking, slow reflexes, and cause drowsiness, unconsciousness, and death. Many people have purchased home monitors to test for carbon monoxide.

▸ *Nitrogen Dioxide* **Nitrogen dioxide** is an amber-colored gas emitted by coal-powered electrical utility boilers and by motor vehicles. High concentrations of nitrogen dioxide can be fatal. Lower concentrations increase susceptibility to colds and flu, bronchitis, and pneumonia. Nitrogen dioxide is also toxic to plant life and causes a brown discoloration of the atmosphere. It is a precursor of ozone, and, along with sulfur dioxide, of acid rain.

▸ *Ozone* Ground-level **ozone** is a form of oxygen that is produced when nitrogen dioxide reacts with hydrogen chloride. These gases release oxygen, which is altered by sunlight to produce ozone. In the lower atmosphere, ozone irritates the mucous membranes of the respiratory system, causing coughing and choking. It can impair lung functioning, reduce resistance to colds and pneumonia, and aggravate heart disease, asthma, bronchitis, and pneumonia. This ozone corrodes rubber and paint and can injure or kill vegetation. It is also one of the irritants found in smog. The natural ozone found in the upper atmosphere (sometimes called "good" ozone), however, serves as a protective membrane against heat and radiation from the sun. We will discuss this atmospheric layer, called the ozone layer, later in the chapter.

▸ *Lead* **Lead** is a metal pollutant that is found in paint, batteries, drinking water, pipes, and dishes with lead-glazed bases. The elimination of lead from gasoline and auto exhaust in the 1970s was one of the great public health accomplishments of all time. Although stricter standards for all of the above prevail, almost 1 million children in the United States had elevated blood lead levels in 1997.[12] Lead affects the circulatory, reproductive, and nervous systems. It can also affect the blood and kidneys and can accumulate in bone and other tissues. Lead is particularly detrimental to children and fetuses. It can cause birth defects, behavioral abnormalities, and decreased learning abilities.

Figure 11.1(a) ■ Example of highlighting and textbook marking.

(continued)

(*Source: Access to Health,* 7th ed. by Rebecca J. Donatelle and Lorraine G. Davis. Copyright © 2002, Pearson Education. Reprinted by permission of Pearson Education, Inc.)

▸ **Hydrocarbons** Although not listed as one of the six major air pollutants in the Clean Air Act, hydrocarbons encompass a wide variety of chemical pollutants in the air. Sometimes known as *volatile organic compounds* (VOCs), **hydrocarbons** are chemical compounds containing different combinations of carbon and hydrogen. The principal source of polluting hydrocarbons is the internal combustion engine. Most automobile engines emit hundreds of different types of hydrocarbon compounds. By themselves, hydrocarbons seem to cause few problems, but when they combine with sunlight and other pollutants, they form such poisons as formaldehyde, various ketones, and peroxyacetylnitrate (PAN), all of which are respiratory irritants. Hydrocarbon combinations such as benzene and benzo(a)pyrene are carcinogenic. In addition, hydrocarbons play a major part in the formation of smog.

••••• **WHAT DO YOU THINK?**

Should automakers be responsible for developing cars with low emissions? As a motorist, how can you help eliminate carbon monoxide emissions?

use as Study Key

Sulfur dioxide A yellowish brown gaseous by-product of the burning of fossil fuels.
Particulates Nongaseous air pollutants.
Carbon monoxide An odorless, colorless gas that originates primarily from motor vehicle emissions.
Nitrogen dioxide An amber-colored gas found in smog; can cause eye and respiratory irritations.
Ozone A gas formed when nitrogen dioxide interacts with hydrogen chloride.
Lead A metal found in the exhaust of motor vehicles powered by fuel containing lead and in emissions from lead smelters and processing plants.
Hydrocarbons Chemical compounds that contain carbon and hydrogen.
Photochemical smog The brownish yellow haze resulting from the combination of hydrocarbons and nitrogen oxides.
Temperature inversion A weather condition occurring when a layer of cool air is trapped under a layer of warmer air.

Photochemical Smog

Photochemical smog is a brown, hazy mix of particulates and gases that forms when oxygen-containing compounds of nitrogen and hydrocarbons react in the presence of sunlight. Photochemical smog is sometimes called *ozone pollution* because ozone is created when vehicle exhaust reacts with sunlight. Such smog is most likely to develop on days when there is little wind and high traffic congestion. In most cases, it forms in areas that experience a **temperature inversion,** a weather condition in which a cool layer of air is trapped under a layer of warmer air, preventing the air from circulating. When gases such as the hydrocarbons and nitrogen oxides are released into the cool air layer, they cannot escape, and thus they remain suspended until wind conditions move away the warmer air layer. Sunlight filtering through the air causes chemical changes in the hydrocarbons and nitrogen oxides, which results in smog. Smog is more likely to be produced in valley regions blocked by hills or mountains—for example, the Los Angeles basin, Denver, and Tokyo.

The most noticeable adverse effects of exposure to smog are difficulty in breathing, burning eyes, headaches, and nausea. Long-term exposure to smog poses serious health risks, particularly for children, the elderly, pregnant women, and people with chronic respiratory disorders such as asthma and emphysema.

Acid Rain

Acid rain is precipitation that has fallen through acidic air pollutants, particularly those containing sulfur dioxides and nitrogen dioxides. This precipitation, in the form of rain, snow, or fog, has a more acidic composition than does unpolluted precipitation. When introduced into lakes and ponds, acid rain gradually acidifies the water. When the acid content of the water reaches a certain level, plant and animal life cannot survive. Ironically, lakes and ponds that are acidified become a crystal-clear deep blue, giving the illusion of beauty and health.

▸ *Sources of Acid Rain* More than 95 percent of acid rain originates in human actions, chiefly the burning of fossil fuels. The single greatest source of acid rain in the United States is coal-fired power plants, followed by ore smelters and steel mills.

When these and other industries burn fuels, the sulfur and nitrogen in the emissions combine with the oxygen and sunlight in the air to become sulfur dioxide and nitrogen oxides (precursors of sulfuric

Figure 11.1(a)   [*continued* in Figure 11.1(b)]

Acid rain has many harmful effects on the environment. Because its toxins seep into groundwater and enter the food chain, it also poses health hazards to humans. (Will and Deni McIntyre/Photo Researchers, Inc.)

acid and nitric acids, respectively). Small acid particles are then carried by the wind and combine with moisture to produce acidic rain or snow. Because of higher concentrations of sunlight in the summer months, rain is more strongly acidic in the summertime. Additionally, the rain or snow that falls at the beginning of a storm is more acidic than that which falls later. The ability of a lake to cleanse itself and neutralize its acidity depends on several factors, the most critical of which is bedrock geology.

▶ *Effects of Acid Rain* The damage caused to lake and pond habitats is not the worst of the problems created by acid rain. Each year, it is responsible for the destruction of millions of trees in forests in Europe and North America. Scientists have concluded that 75 percent of Europe's forests are now experiencing damaging levels of sulfur deposition by acid rain. Forests in every country on the continent are affected.[13]

Doctors believe that acid rain also aggravates and may even cause bronchitis, asthma, and other respiratory problems. People with emphysema and those with a history of heart disease may also suffer from exposure to acid rain. In addition, it may be hazardous to a pregnant woman's unborn child.

Acidic precipitation can cause metals such as aluminum, cadmium, lead, and mercury to **leach** (dissolve and filter) out of the soil. If these metals make their way into water or food supplies (particularly fish), they can cause cancer in humans who consume them.

Acid rain is also responsible for crop damage, which, in turn, contributes to world hunger. Laboratory experiments showed that acid rain can reduce seed yield by up to 23 percent. Actual crop losses are being reported with increasing frequency. A final consequence of acid rain is the destruction of public monuments and structures, with billions of dollars in projected building damage each year.

Indoor Air Pollution

Combating the problems associated with air pollution begins at home. Indoor air can be 10 to 40 times more hazardous than outdoor air. There are between 20 and 100 potentially dangerous chemical compounds in the average American home. Indoor air pollution comes primarily from six sources: woodstoves, furnaces, asbestos, passive smoke, formaldehyde, and radon.

▶ *Woodstove Smoke* Woodstoves emit significant levels of particulates and carbon monoxide in addition to other pollutants, such as sulfur dioxide. If you rely on wood for heating, you should make sure that your stove is properly installed, vented, and maintained. Burning properly seasoned wood reduces the amount of particulates released into the air.

▶ *Furnace Emissions* People who rely on oil- or gas-fired furnaces also need to make sure that these appliances are properly installed, ventilated, and maintained. Inadequate cleaning and maintenance can lead to a buildup of carbon monoxide in the home, which can be deadly.

▶ *Asbestos* **Asbestos** is another indoor air pollutant that poses serious threats to human health. Asbestos is a mineral that was commonly used in insulating materials in buildings constructed before 1970. When bonded to other materials, asbestos is relatively harmless, but if its tiny fibers become loosened and airborne, they can embed themselves in the lungs and cannot be expelled. Their presence leads to cancer of the lungs, stomach, and chest lin-

Figure 11.1(b) ■ Practice sheets for Activity 1. *(continued)*

(*Source: Access to Health,* 7th ed. by Rebecca J. Donatelle and Lorraine G. Davis. Copyright © 2002, Pearson Education. Reprinted by permission of Pearson Education, Inc.)

ing, and is the cause of a fatal lung disease called mesothelioma.

▶ *Formaldehyde*   Formaldehyde is a colorless, strong-smelling gas present in some carpets, draperies, furniture, particle board, plywood, wood paneling, countertops, and many adhesives. It is released into the air in a process called *outgassing*. Outgassing is highest in new products, but the process can continue for many years.

Exposure to formaldehyde can cause respiratory problems, dizziness, fatigue, nausea, and rashes. Long-term exposure can lead to central nervous system disorders and cancer.

To reduce your exposure to formaldehyde, ask about the formaldehyde content of products you purchase and avoid those that contain this gas. Some houseplants, such as philodendrons and spider plants, help clean formaldehyde from the air. If you experience symptoms of formaldehyde exposure, have your home tested by a city, county, or state health agency.

▶ *Radon*   Radon is one of the most serious forms of indoor air pollution. This odorless, colorless gas is the natural by-product of the decay of uranium and radium in the soil. Radon penetrates homes through cracks, pipes, sump pits, and other openings in the foundation. An estimated 30,000 cancer deaths per year have been attributed to radon, making it second only to smoking as the leading cause of lung cancer.[14]

The EPA estimates that 1 in 15 American homes has an elevated radon level. A home-testing kit from a hardware store will enable you to test your home yourself. "Alpha track" detectors are commonly used for this type of short-term testing. They must remain in your home for 2 to 90 days, depending on the device.

▶ *Household Chemicals*   When you use cleansers and other cleaning products, do so in a well-ventilated room, and be conservative in their use. All those caustic chemicals that zap mildew, grease, and other household annoyances cause a major risk to water and the environment. Avoid buildup. Regular cleanings will reduce the need to use potentially harmful substances. Cut down on dry cleaning, as the chemicals used by many cleaners can cause cancer. If your newly cleaned clothes smell of dry-cleaning chemicals, either return them to the cleaner or hang them in the open air until the smell is gone. Avoid the use of household air freshener products containing the carcinogenic agent *dichlorobenzene*.

Indoor air pollution is also a concern in the classroom and workplace. Studies show that one in five U.S. schools has indoor air quality problems, which affect an estimated 8.4 million students.[15] Poor air quality in classrooms may lead to drowsiness, headaches, and lack of concentration. It may also affect physical growth and development. Children with asthma are particularly at risk for adverse health affects from poor air quality.

Each day, many people who work indoors complain of maladies that tend to lessen or vanish when they leave the building. **Sick building syndrome (SBS)** is said to exist when 80 percent of a building's occupants report problems. One of the primary causes of sick building syndrome is poor ventilation. Symptoms include eye irritation, sore throat, queasiness, and worsened asthma.[16]

Acid rain   Precipitation contaminated with acidic pollutants.

Leach   To dissolve and filter through soil.

Asbestos   A substance that separates into stringy fibers and lodges in the lungs, where it can cause various diseases.

Formaldehyde   A colorless, strong-smelling gas released through outgassing; causes respiratory and other health problems.

Radon   A naturally occurring radioactive gas resulting from the decay of certain radioactive elements.

Sick building syndrome (SBS)   Problem that exists when 80 percent of a building's occupants report maladies that tend to lessen or vanish when they leave the building.

Figure 11.1(b)

TAKING NOTES FROM TEXTBOOKS

Taking notes on the material that you've highlighted and marked is necessary for in-depth learning. It would be difficult to have a complete understanding of the material without the notetaking component. When you take notes from your textbook, you add a multi-sensory approach, kinesthetic and visual learning.

Taking notes from printed material is similar to taking notes from a lecture. As you use the SQ3R system, you can write the answers to your questions. Some students like to take notes in their notebook, while others prefer note cards or typing on their computer. You can use any notetaking system. Practice to find the right combination.

ACTIVITIES

Activity 1: Highlighting, Marking, and Notetaking Practice

Directions: Read, highlight, mark, and take notes on the remainder of the health course textbook section on air pollution in this chapter.

Activity 2: More Practice

Directions: Read, highlight, mark, and take notes on the psychology textbook section entitled "The Neurons and the Neurotransmitters" located in Chapter 9. Make study questions. Find a partner and quiz each other.

Activity 3: More Practice

Directions: Read, highlight, mark, and take notes on the psychology textbook section entitled "Introduction to Social Psychology" in Figure 11.2. Create an outline, hierarchy, or mind map after you've taken notes.

INTRODUCTION TO SOCIAL PSYCHOLOGY

Social psychology is the area of study that attempts to explain how the actual, imagined, or implied presence of others influences the thoughts, feelings, and behavior of individuals. No human being lives in a vacuum, alone and apart from other people. We are truly social animals, and our social nature—how we think about, respond to, and interact with other people—provides the territory that social psychology explores. Research in social psychology yields some surprising and provocative answers to puzzling human behavior, from the atrocious to the altruistic.

This chapter explores social perception—how people form impressions of others, and try to understand why they behave as they do. What are the factors involved in attraction? What draws people to one another, and how do friendships and romantic relationships develop? We will look at factors influencing conformity and obedience, and we'll examine groups and their influence on performance and decision making. We will also discuss attitudes and learn how they can be changed, and then we will explore prejudice and discrimination. Finally, we will look at the conditions under which people are likely to help each other (prosocial behavior) and hurt each other (aggression).

To start, let's consider how social psychologists conduct their studies. You may have seen the TV show *Candid Camera*, which showed people "caught in the act of being themselves." Secretly videotaped by a hidden camera, ordinary individuals caught in various social situations provided the humorous, sometimes hilarious, material for the show. This is precisely what researchers in social psychology must do in most of their studies— catch people in the act of being themselves. For this reason deception has traditionally played a prominent part in their research. To accomplish this deception, the researcher often must use one or more **confederates**—people who pose as participants in a psychology experiment but who are actually assisting the experimenter. A **naive subject** is an actual participant who has agreed to participate but is not aware that deception is being used to conceal

social psychology: The study of how the actual, imagined, or implied presence of others influences the thoughts, feelings, and behavior of individuals.

confederate: Someone who is posing as a participant in an experiment but is actually assisting the experimenter.

naive subject: A person who has agreed to participate in an experiment but is not aware that deception is being used to conceal its real purpose.

Figure 11.2 ■ Practice sheets for Activity 3. *(continued)*

(*Source: The World of Psychology*, 4th ed. by Ellen R. Greenwood and Samuel E. Wood. Boston, MA: Allyn and Bacon. Copyright © 2002 by Pearson Education. Reprinted by permission of the publisher.)

primacy effect: The tendency for an overall impression of another to be influenced more by the first information that is received about that person than by information that comes later.

the real purpose of the experiment. Both confederates and naive subjects were used in the Milgram experiment, described at the beginning of this chapter, and you will continue to see why it is often necessary to conceal the purpose of an experiment as you read about other classic studies in social psychology.

SOCIAL PERCEPTION

Are you often surprised by the behavior of other people—the things they say or do? Are you curious about their motives, expectations, or intentions? Other people can be puzzling, but our ability to understand others is important because we live in a social world. The process we use to obtain critically important social information about others is known as *social perception* (Allison et al., 2000).

Impression Formation: Sizing Up the Other Person

When we meet people for the first time, we begin forming impressions about them right away, and, of course, they are busily forming impressions of us. Naturally we notice the obvious attributes first—gender, race, age, dress, and how physically attractive or unattractive someone appears (Shaw & Steers, 2001). Physical attractiveness, as shallow as it might seem, has a definite impact on first impressions. Beyond noticing physical appearance, we may wonder: What is her occupation? Is he married? Answers to such questions, combined with conscious or unconscious assessments of people's verbal and nonverbal behavior, all play their part in forming first impressions. Moods also play a part—when we are happy, our impressions of others are usually more positive than when we are unhappy. And recent research shows that a firm handshake still makes a powerful first impression (Chaplin et al., 2000). It conveys that a person is positive, confident, and outgoing, not shy or weak-willed. Even how frequently people blink their eyes has an impact on the impression they make. Those who blink frequently tend to be rated as more nervous and less intelligent (Omori & Miyata, 1996). First impressions are powerful and can color many of the later impressions we form about people.

What first impression have you formed of the person shown here? (© Charles Gatewood/The Image Works.)

Why are first impressions so important and enduring?

First Impressions: Put Your Best Foot Forward–First If we gave you a list of a certain individual's characteristics or traits and asked you to write your impressions of the person, would it matter which traits were listed first? Solomon Asch (1946) gave one group of participants the following list of traits: intelligent, industrious, impulsive, critical, stubborn, and envious. He then asked the participants to write their impression of the person. Asch gave another group the same list but in reverse order. Participants who responded to the list with the positive traits first gave more favorable evaluations than participants whose list began with the negative traits.

Why should first impressions be so important? A number of studies reveal that an overall impression or judgment of another person is influenced more by the first information received about the person than by information that comes later (Luchins, 1957). This phenomenon is called the **primacy effect**. It seems that we attend to initial information more carefully, and once an impression is formed, it provides the framework through which we interpret later information. Any information that is consistent with the first impression is

Figure 11.2

(continued)

likely to be accepted, thus strengthening the impression. Information that does not fit with the earlier information is more likely to be disregarded.

Remember, any time you list your personal traits or qualities, always list your most positive qualities first. It pays to put your best foot forward—first.

Expectancies: Seeing What You Expect to See Sometimes expectations about how other persons will act in a situation become a self-fulfilling prophecy and actually influence the way they do act. Expectations may be based on a person's gender, age, racial or ethnic group, social class, role or occupation, personality traits, past behavior, relationship to us, and so on. Once formed, our expectancies affect how we perceive the behavior of others—what we pay attention to and ignore. But expectations may also color our attitude and manner toward, and treatment of a person in such a way that we partly bring about the very behavior we expect (Jones, 1986; Miller & Turnbull, 1986).

Attribution: Explaining Behavior

Why do people do the things they do? To answer this question, we all make **attributions**—that is, we assign or attribute causes to explain the behavior of others and to explain our own behavior as well. People are particularly interested in the causes of behaviors when the behaviors are unexpected, when goals are not attained (Weiner, 1985), or when actions are not socially desirable (Jones & Davis, 1965).

Although we can actually observe others' behavior, we can usually only infer its cause or causes. In trying to determine why you or someone else behaved in a certain way, you might make a **situational attribution** (an external attribution) and attribute the behavior to some external cause or factor operating within the situation. After failing an exam, you might say, "The test was unfair" or "The professor didn't give us enough time." Or you might make a **dispositional attribution** (an internal attribution) and attribute the behavior to some internal cause such as a personal trait, motive, or attitude. You might attribute a poor grade to lack of ability or to a poor memory.

Attributional Biases: Different Attributions for Self and Others There are basic differences in the way people make attributions about their own behavior and that of others (Jones, 1976, 1990; Jones & Nisbett, 1971). We tend to use situational attributions to explain our own behavior, because we are aware of factors in the situation that influenced us to act as we did. Also, being aware of our past behavior, we know whether our present actions are typical or atypical.

In explaining the behavior of others, however, people have a consistent tendency to focus more on personal factors than on the factors operating within the situation (Gilbert & Malone, 1995; Leyens et al., 1996). Not knowing how a person has behaved in different situations in the past, we assume a consistency in the behavior. Thus we are likely to attribute the behavior to some personal quality. In the United States, the plight of the homeless and of people on welfare is often attributed to laziness, an internal attribution, rather than to factors in their situation that might explain their condition.

The tendency to attribute our own behavior primarily to situational factors and the behavior of others to internal or dispositional factors is known as the **actor–observer effect.** Members of both Catholic and Protestant activist groups in Northern Ireland are subject to the actor–ob-

---

attribution: An inference about the cause of one's own or another's behavior.

situational attribution: Attributing a behavior to some external cause or factor operating in the situation; an external attribution.

dispositional attribution: Attributing a behavior to some internal cause, such as a personal trait, motive, or attitude; an internal attribution.

actor–observer effect: The tendency to attribute one's own behavior primarily to situational factors and the behavior of others primarily to internal or dispositional factors.

What is the difference between a situational attribution and a dispositional attribution for a specific behavior?

How do the kinds of attributions people tend to make about themselves differ from those they make about other people?

Figure 11.2

(continued)

self-serving bias: The tendency to attribute personal successes to dispositional causes and failures to situational causes.

server effect. Each group attributes the violence of the other group to internal or dispositional characteristics (they are murderers, they have evil intentions, etc.). And each group attempts to justify its own violence by attributing it to external or situational causes (we were just protecting ourselves, we were only retaliating, etc.) (Hunter et al., 2000).

There is one striking inconsistency in the way we view our own behavior: the self-serving bias. We use the **self-serving bias** when we attribute our successes to internal or dispositional causes and blame our failures on external or situational causes (Baumgardner et al., 1986; Brown & Rogers, 1991). If we interview for a job and get it, it is probably because we have the right qualifications. If someone else gets the job, it is probably because he or she knew the right people. The self-serving bias allows us to take credit for our successes and shift the blame for our failures to the situation.

Roesch and Amirkhan (1997) analyzed statements by professional athletes quoted in newspaper articles for evidence of the self-serving bias. And, indeed, athletes did tend to credit their wins to internal factors (their own skills) and to attribute their losses to situational factors (bad luck, poor referees). The self-serving bias was more frequently used by beginning professional athletes than by veterans and by individual athletes (golfers, tennis players) than by members of teams.

Remember It!

1. Which of the following statements about first impressions is *false*?
   a. People usually pay closer attention to early information they receive about a person than to later information.
   b. Early information forms a framework through which other information is interpreted.
   c. First impressions often serve as self-fulfilling prophecies.
   d. The importance of first impressions is greatly overrated.

2. People tend to make _____ attributions to explain their own behavior and _____ attributions to explain the behavior of others.
   a. situational; situational
   b. situational; dispositional
   c. dispositional; situational
   d. dispositional; dispositional

3. The tendency of people to attribute their own behavior primarily to situational factors and the behavior of others primarily to internal causes is called the
   a. actor–observer effect.
   b. false consensus error.
   c. self-serving bias.
   d. external bias error.

4. Attributing Mike's poor grade to his lack of ability is a dispositional attribution. (true/false)

Answers: 1. d 2. b 3. a 4. true

Figure 11.2

CHAPTER 12
Writing Effectively

Inspiration is wonderful when it happens, but the writer must develop an approach for the rest of the time . . . The wait is simply too long.

—Leonard Bernstein, composer

Learning to write effectively not only has great rewards for college success, but for future pursuits as well. In college classes, you develop skills to organize thoughts and ideas to express yourself clearly. The reward is the grade that you receive. After graduation from college, your ability to write effectively continues to be beneficial. Employers prefer hiring people who can produce well-written reports, clear memos, and creative proposals. Good writing skills will serve you throughout your entire lifetime, so it is worth the time and effort it takes to develop them. Stringing words together to make sense seems like it should be easy; the truth is that it can be difficult and frustrating. Luckily, as with any new skill that you are learning, the more you practice, the easier it becomes.

GETTING STARTED: PREWRITING TECHNIQUES

Prewriting literally means "before writing." It's a technique that will help you generate ideas for class assignments, and is the first step in the process of writing an essay, research paper, or speech. It's also an effective tool for getting over "writer's block." When you "brainstorm" or prewrite, you create a variety of ideas from which to choose your final *topic statement* or *thesis*. The basic idea in the process is to relax and let your mind go where it wants to go. This lets you bypass your critical mind (left brain) and discover your creative self. The trick is not to censor yourself or judge. The goal is to generate as many ideas as possible, and no idea is too outrageous or silly. When you do a prewriting exercise, you may find that a number of ideas repeat themselves or that certain patterns emerge in your thinking. Remember that the more ideas you can generate, the more you have to choose from when deciding on a topic. Spending approximately five or ten minutes prewriting will get you started and out of "procrastination mode."

Writers use a preferred style or a combination of prewriting techniques. Experiment with different ones and find the one that is right for you. You may feel more comfortable using a combination of styles.

FREEWRITING

Freewriting involves writing whatever comes into your mind without stopping to evaluate what you've put down on paper or on the computer. Choose your subject and as you write, don't worry about punctuation, grammar, or spelling. Relax and keep writing. You may be surprised at the amount of material that you create. Here's an example of a freewriting about "reality TV."

Reality tv . . . why is it so popular . . . reality shows on every channel about every subject . . . real people—too much reality? . . . currently very trendy. Why??? Shows cheap to produce . . . taking advantage of the public . . . do people care about watching real people rather than actors . . . could I see myself on one of those shows? no, I wouldn't go on one . . . Laughing at other people's flaws, silly antics and behaviors, nosey people, people go on reality shows for love, money, greed, attention, 15 minutes of fame . . . human nature? Interesting to watch.

CLUSTERING OR MIND MAPPING

This right-brain technique (see Chapter 9 on memory) starts with writing the topic or idea in the center of the page and connecting ideas visually in groups or clusters.

Although visual learners prefer creating a mind map to freewriting, no technique is superior; it's simply a matter of choice.

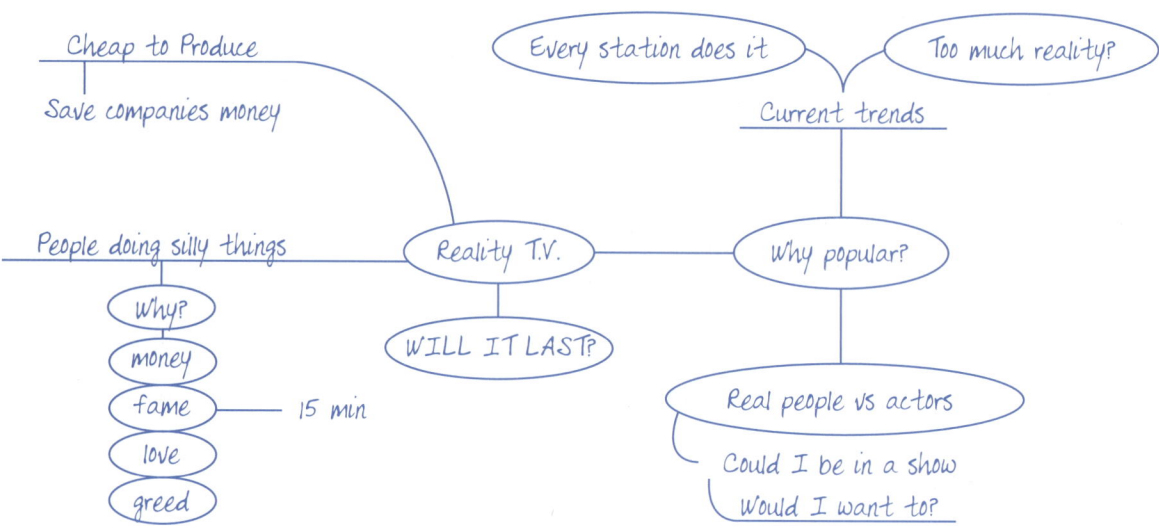

Figure 12.1 ■ Prewriting mind map.

COMBINATION CLUSTERING/FREEWRITING

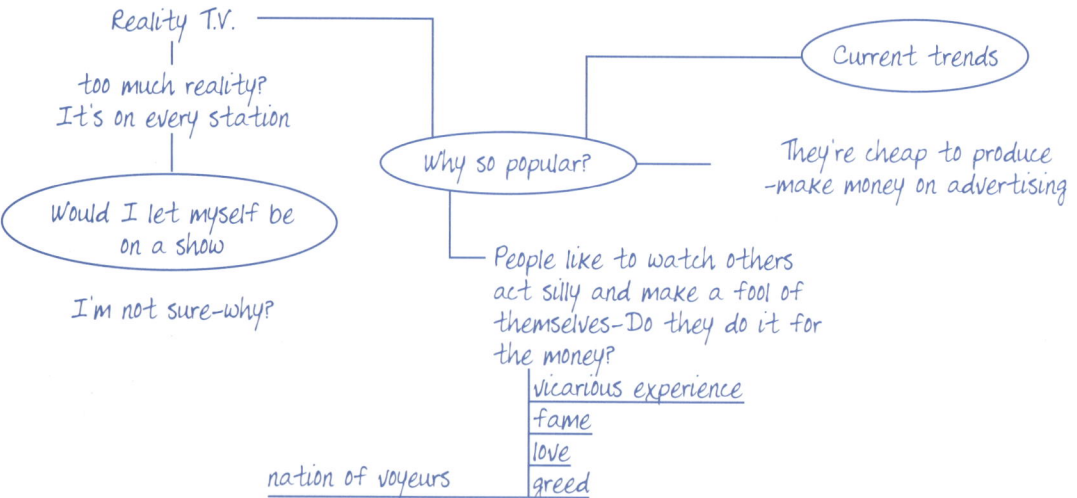

Figure 12.2 ■ Combination of clustering and freewriting.

ELEMENTS OF EFFECTIVE WRITING

As a college student, you will be engaged in several types of writing. You may be asked to respond to a reading assignment with an in-class essay or to answer an essay question as part of an exam. Assigned research papers can vary from short (five to seven pages) to lengthy (ten to fifteen pages). No matter what the essay assignment may be, the basic elements of structure remain the same:

Beginning/Introduction	Middle	End
Thesis statement or topic sentence	Body	Conclusion

BEGINNING/INTRODUCTION

In the opening paragraph, the reader is introduced to the subject of your paper. The main idea, or *thesis statement,* is clearly expressed. Think of this statement as a promise to the reader of what lies ahead. Writing a creative, informative statement will keep your reader interested and wanting to know more about your topic. Create an effective thesis statement by looking over your prewriting exercise and asking the following questions:

- Does one important idea stand out above the rest?
- Are there enough supporting details to support the main idea?

Here are several ideas for thesis statements created from the prewriting exercise about reality TV.

1. Reality TV has captured the imagination of many Americans.
2. The pervasiveness of reality TV makes it seem more popular than it is.
3. Many Americans find reality TV entertaining, although some find it offensive.

Remember that any one of your ideas can benefit from a prewriting exercise.

MIDDLE/BODY

The body of the paper is the "meat" of the paper. The thesis statement is developed with details, facts, opinions, examples, statistics, and/or observations. The way in which you organize information will depend upon the type of assignment you've been given to write. For example, in an argument paper, you would arrange your points from least important to most important, or from general to specific. A paper describing a process would be arranged in chronological order. Be sure to include enough details, examples, or facts to support your thesis statement. Check the coherence of the paper by making sure that each sentence logically follows the one before it. Having someone else read your paper aloud can be beneficial in determining whether the body is developed, unified, and coherent.

END/CONCLUSION

A concluding statement is an important component of effective writing because it sums up the information that you've presented by restating the essay's thesis. It's frustrating when you are engrossed in reading, but then are left hanging by a detail at the end of the essay. It feels unfinished; there is no ending. The busy, thinking, left brain likes completion, and it is your job to provide that for the reader. Because people tend to remember what they read last, you have an opportunity to use powerful language and make an impact.

WRITING RESEARCH PAPERS

Writing a research paper requires gathering and organizing information. The library is an excellent place to begin this process. One reason is that librarians are available to assist you. Not only do they have a wealth of knowledge, but they also know where hard-to-find resources are located. Here are the steps to follow for writing a research paper.

Step 1. **Discover.** Discover sources of information for your topic. These may come from books, periodicals, journals, CD-ROM databases, microfilm, newspapers, audio and videotapes, encyclopedias, and the Internet.

Step 2. **Organize.** Organize your sources. Doing this in the beginning will minimize your stress level. Use 3 × 5 index cards to keep track of your sources, one card for each source. If you are citing books, write the title, author, publisher, edition, year of publication, and the number of pages. For periodicals (magazines), write the title of the article, author's name, title of the magazine, month, year, volume, and relevant page numbers. This information will be used in your bibliography, which shows your instructor the sources you've used for your research paper.

Step 3. **Take notes.** Taking notes for your research can be done in several different ways. Use 3 × 5 cards, and mark each one with a subject heading or key words to keep your ideas organized. As you place them in front of you, you can see the "big" picture. Some students like to use different colored cards for each idea or heading. Another option is to use loose-leaf notebook paper. You can use a separate manila folder for each subject, or categorize by ideas. You may want to have a separate folder for new ideas that pop into your mind while you are researching a subject. A third option is to use a word-processing program. Some students prefer bringing a laptop computer to the library, where they can work in a quiet setting. The library has computers and printers for student use.

Step 4. **Outline.** Make an outline from the information that you have gathered. List headings, subheadings, and supporting details. This will assist you in writing the first draft. *Tip:* Work in the library until you have all of the sources that you need for your research paper. At home, you'll have everything you need in one place and won't have to make an extra trip to the library.

Step 5. **The first draft.** The purpose of the first draft is to get your ideas down on paper. This is a rough draft and is not supposed to be perfect. Don't be too concerned with grammar, punctuation, or spelling at this stage. You will be revising, so it's not necessary to edit while writing the first draft. You will probably write a second or third draft before you write a final one. Putting the paper away for a few days before you write the final draft will give you some distance from it, and a different perspective. This is another reason for not "writing to the deadline."

Step 6. **The final draft.** As you prepare the final draft, review the paper and make final revisions. Proofread your paper carefully.

1. Delete any unnecessary, wordy material.
2. Correct grammar, spelling, and punctuation.
3. Reorganize material as needed.
4. Check that your supporting details support your thesis statement.
5. Read your paper aloud.
6. Ask a friend or writing tutor to read your paper and give you feedback.

Tips for writing research papers:

- **Be sure that you hand in a neatly typed paper.** Use a simple font. Don't get carried away by the fancy and hard-to-read fonts that are in your word-processing programs. A paper that is easy to read is easy to grade.
- **Learn the terms and capabilities of a computer's word-processing program.** *Cutting and pasting* is a valuable editing tool for writing. Most programs have spell checker and grammar checker functions, as well as a dictionary and thesaurus. Use the tutorial program to answer your questions, or take a class at the college. Knowledgeable friends can also be of assistance.
- **Always make a copy of the final paper and keep it in a safe place.** Papers do get lost. Make a photocopy, an extra copy from your printer, or save it on a disc. If you need to produce the paper later for your instructor, you'll be able to do so easily.
- **When using the Web to gather information for research papers,** check the sources carefully. Anyone can create a website; the data presented may be inaccurate or untrue. Check with your instructor or a librarian to validate a particular site. Some instructors provide a list of legitimate authoritative sites for you to use.
- **Don't buy a term paper online and call it your own.** Your instructor will know that you've cheated and automatically fail you. If you can locate a term paper easily, so can your instructor.

Tips for effective writing:

- **Create an environment for writing.** Having a quiet place in which to write helps you organize your thoughts. Soft background music can have a calming effect on nervous writers. Try not to be interrupted. Turn off phones and stay focused.
- **Write a time line or schedule** for completion of your research paper. Divide the tasks into manageable steps. Here's an example:

Monday	Prewrite and create ideas
Tuesday	Decide on a topic and write a thesis statement

Wed–Friday	Research and collect information from the library and Internet
Saturday	Outline and organize paper
Sun–Mon	Work on first draft
Tues–Thursday	Revise first draft
Fri–Sunday	Complete second draft
Mon–Wed	Proofread and complete final draft

Remember to create a realistic time schedule. If you have a workable schedule, you won't be up all night typing your paper the night before it's due. Effective writing requires time to edit, proofread, and correct mistakes.

- **Know your audience.** A paper written for a freshman composition class will require a more formal style than e-mail written to a friend. Ask yourself who will be reading the paper. The use of slang may be acceptable when you're writing an informal letter, but it's not appropriate for college papers. Knowing your audience will help you set the tone of your paper.

Acceptable	Not Acceptable
I don't understand.	I don't get it.
I'm going to . . .	I'm gonna . . .
Kind of	Kinda
Man, hello	Guy, hey

- **Don't plagiarize.** Plagiarizing is copying someone's words and not giving her/him credit for it. Students who get caught plagiarizing may fail a class or be expelled from the college. The consequences don't seem worth the effort it takes to "lift" someone's words and call them your own. Avoid plagiarism by:
- Using quotation marks when you use a person's words. Put them at the beginning and at the end of the quote.
- If you are copying a passage, indent it. If it is six lines or longer, indent it rather than use quotation marks. Use your judgment.
- Keep a record of the publisher, date and page numbers you use on 3 × 5 cards.
- **Use a thesaurus** to increase your vocabulary and to discover new and engaging words for your papers. Keep a dictionary handy to ensure that you are using a word correctly.
- **Be sure that your grammar skills are up to speed.** Buy a usage book or take a grammar class prior to enrolling in freshman composition. Check out the college tutoring and learning center for assistance.
- **Communicate with your instructors** about the writing assignment. Discuss your topic choice. Find out exactly what is expected of you. How long should the paper be? Should it be single or double spaced? One side of the page?
- **Write more than one draft of your paper.** Effective writers write and rewrite. You may need to write your draft several times before you create the one you'll hand in to your instructor.

PREPARING AND PRESENTING ORAL REPORTS

College instructors require students to demonstrate knowledge in a variety of ways. In addition to writing research papers, you may be asked to present an oral report as part of your grade. Whether you are presenting solo or as part of a group, speaking in front of an audience can be a challenge. It's also a first-rate confidence builder. Because many jobs involve giving oral presentations to employers and clients, the public-speaking skills you develop in college contribute to having success in your career.

Tips for preparing oral reports:

- **Pick a topic** in which you have great interest.
- Ask yourself, **"What is the purpose of my talk?"** Know and understand your material.

- **Practice the relaxation** and positive affirmation exercises in this book (Chapters 4 and 5).
- **Use visualization techniques** and imagine that you are a confident speaker. Mentally rehearse your talk before you actually give it.
- **Videotape yourself for practice.** You can time your presentation and critique it.
- **Practice giving your talk** in the mirror or ask family or friends to listen. Ask for feedback.
- **If you are shy or nervous** about speaking in front of an audience, take a speech class.
- **Familiarize yourself with the room** in which you'll be giving your presentation.
- **Prepare an outline** or mind map that you can refer to while you are giving your talk. If you prefer, use 3 × 5 cards and number them to keep them organized.
- **Prepare visual aids.** They will make the material easier to understand. Slides, graphics, and maps are positive additions to your presentation. Check your college's media center to find out what is available for you to use.
- **Use the same structure** in your presentation that you would use in an essay: beginning, middle, and end. Leave the audience with an ending statement that makes an impact. People tend to remember what they've heard last.

Tips for presenting oral reports:
- **Dress for success**; it will help you to feel confident.
- **Your opening sentence** should engage the audience immediately. Some speakers begin with a question, an anecdote, or an interesting quote.
- **Ask a classmate** to signal you if you are going over your allotted time or if you are "losing" the audience. If you feel that you are losing the attention of your audience, take a few steps to one side of the room. Your audience will follow you with their eyes and you'll get their attention back.
- **Make eye contact.** Don't keep looking down to read your notes. If you get nervous, pick a person in the back of the room and direct your presentation to him.
- **Speak loudly and clearly.** You will lose your audience quickly if you mumble.
- **If you lose your place** or feel "frozen," take one step to the right or left, breathe deeply, and begin again.
- **Relax.** When you're relaxed, your audience is relaxed as well.
- **Emphasize words** to keep the audience attentive.

GROUP PRESENTATIONS
- **At the first meeting,** introduce yourself to all of the group members. Decide on your objectives and goals. Create a plan to reach a successful outcome and set up a time for the next meeting.
- **Get together and brainstorm** as many ideas as you can. Remember that this process is creative, so let everyone share his or her ideas. Don't stop or criticize anyone.
- **Divide the tasks** and create a time schedule so that you can achieve your outcome and stay on track. Appoint a timekeeper if necessary.
- **Don't miss a group meeting,** especially if your group meets regularly.
- **If you are the group leader,** be sure that everyone contributes equally. It's your job to keep the group focused.
- **At the end of each group meeting,** evaluate what you have accomplished and decide what the next step will be.
- **Participate enthusiastically** and give everyone a chance.

ACTIVITIES

Activity 1: Checklist for Writers

Directions: Make copies of this checklist and use it for writing assignments.

		Yes	No
1.	I have used prewriting techniques to generate ideas.	___	___
2.	I have created an environment that is conducive to good writing.	___	___
3.	I have outlined my ideas.	___	___
4.	I have decided on a thesis or main idea statement.	___	___
5.	I have completed a time schedule for completing my paper.	___	___
6.	I have determined who my audience is and what kind of language I will use.	___	___
7.	I have an introductory statement in my opening paragraph.	___	___
8.	I have written the first draft of my paper.	___	___
9.	I have included information in the body of my paper necessary to make my points in the form of supporting details, facts, examples, or statistics.	___	___
10.	I have a concluding statement or concluding paragraph.	___	___
11.	I have revised my first draft as many times as necessary.	___	___
12.	I have asked a family member, tutor, or friend to read my paper for feedback.	___	___
13.	I have checked for spelling, grammar, and punctuation errors.	___	___
14.	I have made an extra copy of the paper for myself.	___	___
15.	I have communicated with my instructor, and I know exactly what is expected of me.	___	___

Activity 2: Prewriting Practice

Directions: Practice prewriting for five minutes with each of the following methods: freewrite, clustering/mind map and combination method. Choose from the following subjects:

1. Things that make me:
   angry   confused
   laugh   outspoken
2. Protecting yourself from:
   Internet crime   toxic relationships
   identity theft   illness
3. What would I do if:
   I won the lottery   I earned all As
   I bought a new car I had three wishes

Activity 3: Writing a Thesis Statement

Directions: Select one of your prewriting exercises and answer the following questions to help you create a thesis statement (controlling idea) for your essay.

1. Does one important idea stand out above the rest? If so, what is it? If not, choose another prewriting topic that will generate more ideas.

2. Are there enough supporting details to develop the main idea? If yes, list them. If not, choose another prewriting topic that will generate more ideas.

Review what you've written in Steps 1 and 2 and write a thesis statement.

Activity 4: Oral Presentation

Directions: Give a ten-minute talk to the class. Pick a topic from Activity 2.

CHAPTER 13
Test Taking

A man's errors are his portals of discovery.

—James Joyce, author

TEST ANXIETY: HOW WE DEVELOP FEELINGS OF PANIC

Testing is an integral part of any higher educational system. Tests are given so that you can demonstrate your knowledge and understanding of a subject; the measurement is the grade you earn. The idea of "performing" in a structured setting with time limitations causes stress for many students. This type of stress produces anxiety, which can include symptoms such as nervousness, headaches, sweating, rapid heartbeat, and a sense of panic or dread. A student who experiences any of these symptoms during an exam may "go blank" and forget what she studied. Feelings of helplessness can set in, and the idea of taking another exam produces more anxiety and fear. Why does this happen?

Past experiences: Feelings of panic and dread often originate in the past. Our mind and body remember emotional experiences. A negative experience from the past can trigger an emotional response in the present. Feelings of inadequacy and fear of failure may surface when a person is placed in a stressful situation.

Inadequate preparation: Another reason students feel anxiety when taking a test is that they did not study enough. College exams require depth of information, and often students underestimate the level of the exam questions. When they begin taking the test and realize that they are underprepared, panic sets in.

Tips for minimizing anxiety:

- **Be overprepared.** Nothing builds confidence and reduces anxiety like being overprepared. Some students call this "blue studying," in other words, they study until they're "blue in the face." The following is a technique that will help you become confidently overprepared. It's also a great time-management and memory-improvement skill. Here's how it works:

For example, let's say that you have a psychology class that meets every Monday, Wednesday, and Friday at 9:00 A.M. On Monday, sometime after class, read the notes that you took that day. Don't try to memorize them; just read them with focused attention. On Tuesday, read the notes that you took in Monday's class. On Wednesday, read the notes that you took on Monday and Wednesday. On Thursday, read the notes from Monday and Wednesday. On Friday, read the notes that you have from Monday, Wednesday, and Friday. Do the same on Saturday and Sunday. Don't skip the weekend. Find a few minutes to read your notes every day. Fit it into your schedule. Let's say that the first psychology exam is scheduled three weeks into the term. How many times have you read Monday's notes? The answer is 21 times. Wednesday's notes? 19 times. Friday's notes? 17. Do you think you that you will know the material in your notes?

Monday	Tuesday	Wednesday	Thursday	Friday	Saturday	Sunday
Psychology class: Take notes Read notes	Read Monday's notes	Take notes in Psychology class Read notes from Monday and Wednesday	Read notes from Monday and Wednesday	Take notes in Psychology class Read notes from Monday, Wednesday, and Friday	Read notes from Monday, Wednesday, and Friday	

Figure 13.1 ■ Notetaking chart.

This technique doesn't take much time, perhaps a few minutes per day. It works by using repetition and visual memory. You won't have to cram for an exam because you are prepared. Use this technique with all of your class material. See above chart, Figure 13.1.

- **Use relaxation techniques.** Try the progressive relaxation exercises suggested in this book. Let your deep breaths relax your muscles and send oxygen to your brain. Practice the techniques for a few minutes each day; when you do them before taking an exam, you'll be able to relax easily and remember what you know.
- **Use positive self-affirmations.** Give positive messages to your subconscious mind. Say these affirmations with deep breaths right before you take an exam, such as, "I am remembering everything I have studied, I am focused and relaxed, and information is available to me," or "I am answering all of the questions with ease."

PREPARATION FOR TEST TAKING

Preparation for taking tests involves using learning strategies and effective time management. There is no one "right" way to prepare; in fact, using a combination of techniques provides a variety of ways to store information into your LTM.

Tips to help you prepare for taking exams:

- **Devise a study plan.** Decide how many hours per day that you will devote to studying for your exam. Begin an intensive review at least one week before the exam date. Be realistic in setting time goals.
- **Divide your time.** Remember to study in "manageable chunks" of time. Take breaks if you feel fatigued. Don't forget to stand, stretch, and move around.
- **Study with a partner or in a group.** Reviewing with another person or a group can give you valuable feedback and identify the "holes" in your knowledge. "Talking the material" helps you learn it. Quiz each other. Create your own tests and exchange them.
- **Find out about the exam.** Ask your instructor to give you information about the kind of questions that he will ask. Will there be essay, true/false, or multiple-choice questions, or a combination of these? Will the exam be open or closed book? Be sure to know what chapters will be covered and if you will be tested on additional sources of information. Students are sometimes shy about asking questions or feel that they don't have a right to ask, but the more that you learn about the exam, the more you can focus your study sessions. Remember that the least helpful response to the question, "What will be on the test?" is, "Study everything!" You have nothing to lose by asking.
- **Study handouts that are given out by the instructor.** Handouts provide additional information to your text and provide good test material.
- **Ask your instructor to hand out a study guide.** A study guide tells you what the instructor thinks is important.

- **Obtain copies of previous tests used by the instructor.** Sometimes tests are on file in the department office and can be checked out. The instructor may keep a file in her office as well. Talk to friends and students who've taken the class; they can give you input and study hints.
- **Create study aids.** Study aids can include outlines, flash cards, hierarchies, summaries, and mind maps. Combine the ones that work best for you. Use the cue column from your Cornell notes or the Leonard system 5 × 7-inch cards to study.
- **Recite information into a tape recorder.** Make your own study tape and listen to it when you're in your car or riding the bus or subway. Listen to it right before you go to bed at night. The information will be the last thing you hear before you drift off to sleep.
- **Make up your own test.** What would you ask your students if you were the instructor? What would you expect them to know? Take your own test and then use it as a study guide.
- **Always attend the class the day before an exam.** This is essential! The instructor may give last-minute information about the test or give hints related to test questions. It is a mistake to take this day off in order to study. The time is better spent attending class. It could mean the difference in your grade.

PUTTING YOUR SKILLS TO WORK: SUCCEEDING ON EXAMS

Success strategies to use before taking an exam:

- **Get plenty of sleep the night before the exam.** Being well rested will help you think clearly and be alert.
- **Eat breakfast the day of the exam.** Foods that contain protein and that are low in sugar will keep your concentration at an optimum level. "Break fast" literally means that you are breaking the fast from a night of sleeping. Your body needs to know that you are awake, and eating breakfast will provide the signal.
- **Set your alarm one-half hour early the day of the exam.** You'll have extra time to review your study notes.

Success strategies for taking exams:

- **Preview the test before you take it.** This will give you an overall view of what's on the test. It's worth a few minutes of your time to get the big picture. How many questions are on the test? What type are they? What is their point value? Will you need extra paper to answer a question? How much time will you have to do the exam?
- **Look at the clock.** You will want to budget your time. How much will you need for each section? Get a clear idea of how you will divide your time. You want to make sure that you have enough time to complete the exam.
- **Read the directions carefully and slowly.** Circle important direction words. If the true/false section asks you to mark "O" for false, and you write "F," your answers will be marked wrong. If the multiple-choice section asks you to circle the "best" answer, it isn't necessarily asking you for the "correct" answer. Essay questions also have specific direction words that are important to read with care.
- **Do what you know first.** Begin the exam by answering the questions that you are sure of. This is a confidence booster. Imagine how you would feel if you started with question number 1 and couldn't answer the next four questions. Don't let self-doubt sneak in. Start with the easy questions and work your way to the difficult ones.
- **Use all of the time that is allotted for the exam.** It is a good idea to take time to review your answers before you hand in your paper. Because test taking can be stressful, students want to finish and leave. Even if you finish your test early, take the extra time to make sure that you've answered every question to the best of your ability. You may discover that you've left an answer

blank or have forgotten to do a part of the test. If you sit quietly for awhile, instead of rushing to leave the room, an answer you think you can't remember might come to you.

- **Trust your first response.** Studies show that the first answer you choose tends to be correct. Trust your "gut feeling" and don't change an answer unless you are sure that you are changing it to the correct one.

- **Answer every exam question.** It is better to guess than to leave a question unanswered. Usually, an answer that is left blank will be marked wrong. If you are not sure of the answer to a question, leave it blank and make a mark, * or →, next to it. Keep the question in mind as you proceed. You might find the answer in another part of the exam. This happens often because it's easy to overlap material when writing an exam. Remember to go back to the question that you left unanswered. If you still don't know the answer, use the strategies in this book suggested for "educated guessing." Be careful when taking tests using scantrons (a machine-corrected test). A stray mark can become an incorrect answer.

SUBJECTIVE AND OBJECTIVE EXAMS

College exams usually consist of a combination of objective and subjective questions. *Objective tests* consist of true/false, matching, multiple-choice, and fill-in-the-blank questions. Objective tests give you choices and clues from which to recognize the correct answer.

Subjective tests consist of essay questions, the answers of which will vary in length from one paragraph to several pages. This type of test asks you to recall, organize, and present information in a well-written form.

Students tend to develop a preference for subjective or objective testing. Those who are good at recalling facts and details, and who enjoy "educated guessing," generally prefer objective tests. On the other hand, students who like writing and organizing material have a preference for short-answer and essay tests. Regardless of student preference, preparation for both types is essential.

ANSWERING TRUE/FALSE QUESTIONS

The best course of action for taking any exam is to know the material well. This allows you to move through the exam quickly, feeling confident in your choice of answers. The following tips are to help you make "educated guesses" when you're not certain of the answer.

- **Read through the question carefully.** For the answer to be true, every part of the question must be true. One incorrect option can make the answer false. Here's an example:

    Howard Gardner's Theory of Multiple Intelligence includes linguistic, musical, interpersonal, contextual, and naturalistic types of intelligence. T or F.
    The answer is *false*. All the types of intelligence listed fit the theory except "contextual," which is not part of Gardner's theory. One word changed the sentence from being true to false.

- If you do not know the answer to a question and you decide to guess, guess TRUE. You have a 50 percent chance of choosing the correct answer. Instructors tend to put more true questions in tests.

- **Pay attention to 100 percent qualifying words.** Because these words state absolutes, they tend to be found in FALSE statements. Examples of 100 percent qualifiers are **all, always, never, only, none, invariably, no one.**

    All children play soccer. (false)

    The *only* time I sleep is when I'm tired. (false)

- Qualifying words that are not 100 percent tend to be found in TRUE statements. Examples of these words are **frequent, sometimes, often, many, most, may usually.**

    Many children play soccer. (true)

    I *sometimes* sleep when I'm tired. (true)

- **Pay attention to questions that state reasons.** They tend to be false because they state an incorrect reason, or they don't state all of them. Here is an example:

  The reason many young women have eating disorders is that they are overly concerned with their physical appearance. T or F.

  The answer is *false*. While this may be one of the reasons that women have eating disorders, it is not the only one. To help you determine whether the statement is true or false, read "the reason" as "the only reason."

- **Pay attention to negatives.** Negative words in true/false statements can be difficult and require careful reading. They are easy to miss, and can confuse the meaning of a sentence. Circle the negatives before you read. Examples are **no, not, and none. Watch for words that contain negative prefixes.** Circle them first, and then read the sentence carefully. Examples are **un, non, dis, ir, il, in, im, un.**

  *Un*breakable = not breakable
  *non*compliant = not compliant
  *dis*agreeable = not agreeable
  *ir*replaceable = not replaceable
  *il*literate = not literate
  *in*valid = not valid
  *im*practical = not practical
  *un*finished = not finished

- **Identify double negatives.** Double negatives are statements that include two negatives in a sentence, usually the word "not" and a prefix. The rule to follow is that two negatives = a positive. Cross out both negatives and read your statement to determine whether it is true or false. Here's an example:

  Coffee is ~~not~~ a ~~non~~alcoholic beverage. T or F.

  The sentence now reads: Coffee is a(n) alcoholic beverage. The answer is FALSE.

  Fine china is ~~not un~~breakable. T or F.

  The sentence now reads: Fine china is breakable. The answer is TRUE.

ANSWERING MULTIPLE-CHOICE QUESTIONS

A multiple-choice question asks you to complete a statement. The incomplete part of the statement is called the *stem,* and the choices from which to choose a correct answer are called the *options*. Like true/false, multiple choice questions need to be read carefully. In answering multiple-choice questions, always do what you know first. If you are not sure of the answer, make an "educated guess" using the following strategies.

- Eliminate 100 percent qualifiers as options. Example:

  The short term memory:
     a. *always* stores new information
     b. holds five to seven items at a time
     c. *only* holds sensory information
     d. is *never* accurate in remembering

  Letters a, c, and d all have 100 percent qualifiers. Once you have eliminated them as choices, b remains, which is the correct answer.

- Choose "all of the above" as the correct choice. Example:

  Hypnosis has been used successfully for:
     a. smoking cessation
     b. changes in perception and feeling
     c. pain control
     d. all of the above

  Letter d is the correct answer.

- When asked to choose a number, eliminate the highest and lowest and choose the middle one. Example:

  A football game is played on a field measuring:
  a. 150 yards
  b. 100 yards
  c. 90 yards (eliminate lowest)
  d. 200 yards. (eliminate highest)

  You now have a 50 percent chance deciding between options a and b. The correct answer is b.

- Choose your answer from similar-looking options. Example:

  A major cause of stroke is:
  a. low blood pressure
  b. high blood pressure
  c. poor diet
  d. increased HDL cholesterol

  Choose between letters a and b. The correct answer is b.

- Discard foolish or silly options, jokes, insults, or unfamiliar terms. Example:

  If you are suffering from stress, you should:
  a. yell at everyone
  b. see a counselor
  c. sleep 24 hours per day
  d. see a phlebotomist

  Option a is not an appropriate behavior, c is an unrealistic choice, and d is probably an unfamiliar term. The correct answer is b.

- Choose the most inclusive answer. Example:

  Theories of motivation include:
  a. Instinct Theory
  b. Drive Reduction Theory
  c. Stimulus Theory
  d. a and b

  The correct answer is d, which includes both a and b.

- Read the stem of each question and option separately, as you would a true/false question. Example:

  The most common type of objective test is:
  a. true and false
  b. multiple choice
  c. fill-in
  d. short-answer completion

  a. The most common type of objective test is true or false. T or F
  b. The most common type of objective test is multiple choice. T or F
  c. The most common type of objective test is fill-in. T or F
  d. The most common type of objective test is short-answer completion. T or F

  The correct answer is b. This is an excellent technique when you feel "stuck."

SENTENCE COMPLETION AND FILL-IN

Sentence completion and fill-in-the-blank questions ask you to complete missing information. Here are some strategies for taking this type of test.

- **Think about definitions and key words** that might fit into your sentence. Think logically. Here's a challenge: try to think the way your instructor thinks.
- **Ask specific questions** to clarify your understanding of the sentences you are to complete.

- **Pay attention** to the grammatical structure of a sentence. If "a" is used before a blank space, the next word will begin with a consonant. If "an" is used, the next word will begin with a vowel.
- **Notice the length and number of blanks and spaces.** If you are not sure if more than one word is required, ask your instructor for clarification.
- **Be creative.** Even if you are not writing the exact required answer, you may get some points for your creativity.

STRATEGIES FOR ESSAY EXAMS

Essay tests ask you to recall and organize information. This type of exam asks more of you than the objective type. No recognition clues are given. You are required to answer a question in depth within a specific time frame. Mastery of the material is essential. *Here are strategies to use:*

- **Read the questions carefully.** These types of questions use an organizational prompt or *guide word* to help you focus the direction of your answer. Even though you may know the material well, you can lose valuable points on the test if you don't answer what is specifically being asked of you.
- **Circle the guide word** in the question as you read it. Before you begin writing, reread it to make sure that you're on the right track. Here is a list of guide words and their meanings.

Guide Word	Meaning
Analyze	Separate into parts and discuss in detail.
Compare	Explain similarities and differences.
Contrast	Explain differences only.
Define	State the definition or meaning.
Describe	Give as many details as possible. Use multisensory language.
Discuss	State pros and cons. Use supporting details and examples.
Evaluate	Give your opinion and support it with reasons, facts, and examples.
Explain	Give reasons and examples.
Illustrate	Give examples.
Justify	Prove: give examples as evidence of your argument.
List or Enumerate	List information using numbers or a series of items.
State	Explain briefly and concisely.
Summarize	Review the main ideas.
Trace	Follow events in chronological order. Give a history from beginning to end.

- If your exam has both objective and subjective questions, **read the essay question before you do the objective part.** Keep the question in mind as you do the multiple-choice or true/false sections. You will likely pick up information that you can use in writing your essay.
- **Plan and strategize.** Planning is an important part of writing an effective essay. Strategize by doing a quick analysis. As soon as you read the question, identify points that you want to make. Use a hierarchy or outline to jot down facts and notes that you want to include. You can add to it while you take other parts of the exam. Planning creates good time management. Budget your time to minimize stress, and you'll have the time you need to write a thoughtful, effective essay.
- If you know that you will not have enough time to complete your essay, **write an outline or list the points** that you had planned to make. This shows the instructor that the reason that your essay was not complete was because of a lack of time, not knowledge. Add a short note of

explanation to the instructor. You may earn points even though your entire answer wasn't in complete sentences.

WRITING THE ESSAY

When writing your essay, you want to be as clear and concise as possible. Begin by determining the required length of the assignment. If you're not sure, ask your instructor.

- Use the following organizational form:
  Beginning—Thesis or main idea statement
  Middle—Body of the essay
  End—Conclusion
- **Use key words** from the essay question in your opening or thesis sentence. If you are "stuck" and not sure of how to begin your essay, omit the guide word and use the key words in the question. Here's an example:
  Question: Discuss the characteristics of creative people.
  Your opening sentence: Creative people share a number of characteristics.
  The *middle* is the body of your essay. It consists of supporting details, facts, and examples. Develop your examples with secondary detail. Write in complete sentences. Check to be sure that one sentence logically follows another. Think of yourself as a lawyer presenting evidence. Are you making a convincing case for the jury?
- **Assume that your reader** (in this case, the instructor) does not know much about your subject. This technique will help you explain things clearly and not leave out any important steps.
- **Underline your main ideas.** This will make grading easier for the instructor. Remember that clear organization is essential for an essay to be effective.
- **Be neat.** If your paper is easy to read, it's easy to grade. Use pen rather than pencil. Bring a spell checker to class to correct spelling errors.
- **Write on one side of the page.** If your writing "bleeds through" to the other side of the paper, it will be difficult to read.
- **Don't put your personal opinion** in the essay unless you are specifically asked for it. Check the guideword list. The words evaluate, criticize, and interpret ask for your opinion.
- Leave blank spaces for adding "late" ideas.

ACTIVITIES

Activity 1: Writing a Test

Directions: Create a sample objective test. Write ten true/false questions and five multiple-choice questions. Use the information presented in this chapter to construct your test. Exchange tests with a partner and total your score.

Activity 2: Creating Essay Questions

Directions: Select a chapter from this text and write three essay questions related to the material. Choose one to answer in class for practice.

Activity 3: Understanding Test-Taking Strategies

Directions: Create an outline, mind map, or hierarchy of the test-taking strategies that you will use both before and during a test.

CHAPTER 13: TEST TAKING

Never give up!

Figure 13.2

Appendix:
Time Management Forms

The blank forms in this appendix are for you to use throughout the school year. Make copies of them to keep track of homework assignments and to create time-management schedules.

Name _____

Data Gathering

Time	Monday	Tuesday	Wednesday	Thursday	Friday	Saturday	Sunday
6–7							
7–8							
8–9							
9–10							
10–11							
11–12							
12–1							
1–2							
2–3							
3–4							
4–5							
5–6							
6–7							
7–8							
8–9							
9–10							
10–11							
11–12							
12–1							

Weekly Schedule

Time	Monday	Tuesday	Wednesday	Thursday	Friday	Saturday	Sunday
6–7							
7–8							
8–9							
9–10							
10–11							
11–12							
12–1							
1–2							
2–3							
3–4							
4–5							
5–6							
6–7							
7–8							
8–9							
9–10							
10–11							
11–12							
12–1							

Weekly Schedule

Time	Monday	Tuesday	Wednesday	Thursday	Friday	Saturday	Sunday
6–7							
7–8							
8–9							
9–10							
10–11							
11–12							
12–1							
1–2							
2–3							
3–4							
4–5							
5–6							
6–7							
7–8							
8–9							
9–10							
10–11							
11–12							
12–1							

Weekly Schedule

Time	Monday	Tuesday	Wednesday	Thursday	Friday	Saturday	Sunday
6–7							
7–8							
8–9							
9–10							
10–11							
11–12							
12–1							
1–2							
2–3							
3–4							
4–5							
5–6							
6–7							
7–8							
8–9							
9–10							
10–11							
11–12							
12–1							

Daily Schedule

8	
9	
10	
11	
12	
1	
2	
3	
4	
5	
6	
7	

Assignment Sheet

Name _____   Week of _____

Course Name	Monday date:	Tuesday date:	Wednesday date:	Thursday date:	Friday date:

Assignment Sheet

Week of _____

Date	Due	Class	Assignment	Done

_____
_____
_____
_____
_____
_____